KNOW YOUR ENEMIES

A Biblical Theology of Satan, the Flesh, and the World

DR. JEAN MARC JOSEPH

Know Your Enemies
A Biblical Theology of Satan, the Flesh, and the World
By Dr. Jean Marc Joseph • Copyright © 2026
All rights reserved.

Unless otherwise noted, all Scripture quotations are taken from THE HOLY BIBLE, NEW INTERNATIONAL VERSION®, NIV® Copyright © 1973, 1978, 1984, 2011 by Biblica, Inc.® Used by permission. All rights reserved worldwide.

Scripture quotations marked (ESV) are from the ESV Bible® (The Holy Bible, English Standard Version®), copyright © 2001 by Crossway Bibles, a publishing ministry of Good News Publishers. Used by permission. All rights reserved.

Published by:
Dr. Jean Marc Joseph
Atlanta, Georgia, USA
www.EvangelistJeanMarc.org

ISBN: 979-8-9954075-0-8

Cover and book design by:
Exodus Design Studio
www.ExodusDesign.com

First Edition, 2026
Printed in the United States of America

DEDICATION

To the church of Jesus Christ,

called to be strong in the Lord and in the strength

of His might, to stand firm against the schemes of the devil,

to walk in truth and holiness according to His Word,

and to overcome by the blood of the Lamb

and the word of their testimony.

May this work equip those

who put on the whole armor of God

and remain steadfast until the final victory

of Christ is revealed.

EPIGRAPH

*"Be sober-minded; be watchful. Your adversary the devil prowls around
like a roaring lion, seeking someone to devour.
Resist him, firm in your faith."*
— 1 Peter 5:8–9

*"For all that is in the world, the desires of the flesh and the desires of
the eyes and pride of life, is not from the Father but is from the world."*
— 1 John 2:16

*"They have conquered him by the blood of the Lamb and by the word of
their testimony, for they loved not their lives even unto death."*
— Revelation 12:11

*"This life, therefore, is not righteousness but growth in righteousness;
not health but healing; not being but becoming; not rest but exercise."*
— Martin Luther

"Where God builds a church, there the devil builds a chapel."
— Martin Luther

TABLE OF CONTENTS

PREFACE

The Scriptures present salvation as deliverance from sin, death, and the dominion of darkness. Yet many believers lack a biblical framework for understanding spiritual warfare. Some attribute every struggle to Satan, while others deny his influence entirely. Scripture affirms neither extreme. Instead, it reveals a sober, Christ-centered realism: the enemy is real, defeated, active, and limited by divine sovereignty.

Views concerning Satan are often shaped more by imagination than by Scripture. New Testament scholar D. A. Carson, in *Exegetical Fallacies*, warns against word-study errors in which interpreters assume that "the meaning of a word in a specific context may bring with it the word's entire semantic range."[1] Carson further explains that interpreters err when they treat a word's full semantic range as though it were present in every occurrence, rather than allowing context to determine its specific meaning.

This book restores biblical balance by grounding spiritual warfare firmly in Christology[2], soteriology[3], and eschatology[4]. In

---

[1] D. A. Carson, *Exegetical Fallacies*, 2nd ed. (Grand Rapids: Baker Academic, 1996), 60.

[2] Christology is the branch of theology that studies the person and work of Jesus Christ, including His divine and human natures, His incarnation, His sinless life, His atoning death, His resurrection, and His ongoing mediatorial reign.

keeping with the aim articulated by evangelical theologian Wayne Grudem in Systematic Theology, this work likewise seeks to restore a more biblical balance to discussions of doctrine by emphasizing the teaching of the whole of Scripture rather than reliance on any single theological system."[5] The aim of this book is not to inspire fear, but to establish truth.

New Testament scholar Gordon D. Fee, in Pauline Christology, emphasizes that Paul does not construct a formal, argued Christology but rather presupposes Christ's lordship throughout his writings."[6] This insight is directly relevant for understanding spiritual warfare in Paul: Christ's lordship is not constructed within the conflict but presupposed as its foundation. The believer does not fight for victory, but from the victory already secured in Christ through His incarnation, atoning death, resurrection, and exaltation. The cross stands at the center of this reality: victory is secured not by human effort but by Christ's substitutionary death and resurrection. In The Theology of the Book of Revelation (1993), Richard Bauckham writes that "by juxtaposing the two contrasting images, John has forged a new symbol of conquest by sacrificial death."[7] (See Chapters 1 and 18.) This statement, situated within his exposition of Revelation 5, shows that the Lamb (Revelation

---

[3] Soteriology is the doctrine of salvation, examining how God redeems sinners through the work of Christ and applies that redemption by the Holy Spirit.

[4] Eschatology is the study of the last things, focusing on the culmination of God's redemptive plan, including the return of Christ, final judgment, resurrection, and the establishment of the new heavens and new earth.

[5] Wayne Grudem, *Systematic Theology: An Introduction to Biblical Doctrine* (Grand Rapids, MI: Zondervan, 1994).

[6] Gordon D. Fee, *Pauline Christology: An Exegetical-Theological Study* (Peabody, MA: Hendrickson, 2007).

[7] Richard Bauckham, *The Theology of the Book of Revelation* (Cambridge: Cambridge University Press, 1993), 65.

5:6) reinterprets the Lion (Revelation 5:5), thereby defining victory through sacrificial witness.

To know the enemy is not to glorify him, fear him, or obsess over his schemes, but to recognize his nature, methods, and limitations as Scripture reveals. Satan is neither an equal rival to God nor a mere metaphor for evil. He is a created being, fallen and judged, whose authority is temporary and whose defeat is certain. Believers are therefore called neither to panic nor passivity, but to vigilance rooted in truth.

Just as important, spiritual warfare must never be reduced to the study of demons alone. The biblical witness identifies three interrelated adversaries: the devil, the flesh, and the world. An overemphasis on external spiritual forces often obscures the internal struggle against indwelling sin and the subtle pressures of a fallen world system. Authentic warfare must address all three enemies within the unified framework of redemption.

A unified framework explains why salvation must address multiple enemies:

- **Satan** – defeated through Christ's victory

- **The flesh** – transformed through regeneration and sanctification

- **The world** – overcome through allegiance to God's kingdom

A unified framework of redemption understands Scripture as a single, coherent narrative in which God progressively reveals and accomplishes His saving purposes through Christ, addressing sin, evil, and disorder in both personal and cosmic dimensions until final restoration is complete.

This book is not to sensationalize spiritual conflict, but to train the church in discernment, maturity, and steadfast faith. Spiritual warfare is not about dramatic confrontations, but about daily obedience, renewed minds, disciplined lives, and unwavering allegiance to Christ. Victory happens not through extraordinary experiences, but through perseverance in holiness, truth, and love.

This study directs the reader away from fear and toward confidence. This confidence is not in human strength, techniques, or formulas, but in the supremacy of Christ and the authority of His Word. When believers understand who Christ is, what He has accomplished, and where they stand in Him, the enemy's power is exposed for what it is: real, but broken.

May this work serve the church by equipping believers to stand firm, think biblically, and live victoriously until the final consummation, when the defeated enemy is forever removed, and Christ reigns openly as all in all.

Acknowledgments

Above all, I give thanks to the sovereign and gracious God Almighty, who placed this burden and vision upon my heart. In His perfect timing, He has brought it to completion. This work was written in obedience to His call, that His people might see clearly, turn from darkness to light, and from the power of Satan to God, receiving forgiveness of sins and an inheritance among those sanctified by faith in Jesus Christ (Acts 26:18).

I am profoundly thankful to God for my wife and our two daughters. Their prayers, patience, and encouragement have been a constant source of strength throughout this journey, and I do not take their support lightly.

I also extend my sincere gratitude to my editor and formatter, whose careful guidance, clarity of insight, and thoughtful editorial work in editing, formatting, and typesetting helped shape this manuscript into its final form. Their commitment to excellence has strengthened both the readability and the faithfulness of this work.

To God alone be all glory. May this book serve the church in truth, discernment, and steadfast hope until the day of our Lord Jesus Christ.

INTRODUCTION

THE REALITY OF THE BATTLEFIELD

Eden, Exile, and the Enemies of God's Dwelling—A Canonical Framework for Spiritual Warfare

We cannot understand biblical spiritual warfare apart from the unified storyline of Scripture. From Genesis to Revelation, the Bible presents a coherent narrative centered on God's plan to dwell with humanity in holiness and peace. The enemies confronting the people of God—Satan, the flesh, and the world—are not isolated phenomena but emerge within the broader redemptive-historical drama of Scripture. Old Testament scholar T. Desmond Alexander, in From Eden to the New Jerusalem, demonstrates that Scripture unfolds as a unified narrative moving from the original sacred space of Eden to the eschatological reality of the New Jerusalem, revealing a continuous divine purpose centered on the restoration of God's dwelling with His people.[8] This framework provides the theological blueprint upon which the present study of spiritual warfare is built.

The New Testament often employs the language of conflict, battle, wrestle, struggle, resistance, fight, armor, vigilance, strongholds, and victory to describe the Christian life. Spiritual warfare is not metaphorical rhetoric but a reality. The apostle Paul

---

[8] T. Desmond Alexander, *From Eden to the New Jerusalem: An Introduction to Biblical Theology* (Grand Rapids, MI: Kregel Publications, 2008).

exhorts believers: "Put on the full armor of God, so that you can take your stand against the devil's schemes. For our struggle is not against flesh and blood, but against the rulers, against the authorities, against the powers of this dark world and against the spiritual forces of evil in the heavenly realms." (Ephesians 6:11–12).

This summons calls believers to spiritual preparedness rooted not in human strength but in divine provision. The conflict is not physical but spiritual, requiring discernment, endurance, and dependence upon God.

Scripture identifies three distinct yet interconnected enemies every believer faces:

1 **Satan and the demons** — the external personal spiritual adversary.

2 **The flesh** — the internal fallen human nature.

3 **The world** — the external system opposed to God.

For clarity, these three enemies are treated in sequence: Satan (Chapter 3), the flesh (Chapter 11), and the world system (Chapter 18). Mistaking the enemy leads to doctrinal confusion, misplaced blame, and being vulnerable to deception. As the prophet declares, "My people are destroyed for lack of knowledge" (Hosea 4:6).

As the ancient strategist Sun Tzu observes in The Art of War, "If you know the enemy and know yourself, you need not fear the result of a hundred battles." While not a biblical source, this principle illustrates a truth that Scripture affirms in a deeper and ultimate sense."[9]

---

[9] Sun Tzu, *The Art of War,* trans. Samuel B. Griffith (Oxford: Oxford University Press, 1963), chap. 3.

This principle indicates that a comprehensive understanding of both the enemy and oneself is essential for effective engagement. When one discerns the enemy's strengths, weaknesses, strategies, and limitations, and likewise understands one's own capabilities, vulnerabilities, resources, and discipline, the conditions for consistent success are established. Victory, therefore, is not accidental but the result of informed and deliberate preparation.

While not derived from Scripture, this observation reflects a pattern consistent with biblical wisdom. In the spiritual realm, believers who rightly understand both the strategies of the adversary and their own identity and authority in Christ are equipped to stand firm without fear.

The apostle Peter exhorts the church: "Be sober-minded and alert. Your adversary the devil prowls around like a roaring lion looking for someone to devour. Resist him, standing firm in the faith" (1 Peter 5:8–9).

Many believers proclaim victory while remaining unaware of the enemies that oppose them. Many people neither acknowledge nor understand Satan and demonic forces. Yet life's pressures and trials, whether spiritual, moral, cultural, or relational, are not random. They are rooted in the ongoing opposition believers encounter on their earthly journey. This conflict does not cease; it continues until the believer enters eternal life.

Without discernment of the enemy's methods, God's people remain exposed and unprepared. Therefore, we must recognize Christians are confronted by three distinct adversaries who never cease in their efforts.

Views of Satan are often shaped more by ideas than by Scripture. Some reduce him to folklore; others interpret him as a symbolic figure, and still others view him as an impersonal force capable of shifting forms. Such distortions obscure biblical understanding and weaken spiritual discernment. The Christian struggle is not waged against human opponents, but against the three enemies we examine in this book. We achieve true victory only by understanding, through Christ and the authority of Scripture, how to resist and defeat these forces.

This study begins with the chief adversary: Satan, the devil. Scripture provides clear insight into his identity, methods, schemes, and limitations.

We can't avoid spiritual warfare in the Christian life. Daily pressures, whether internal or external, moral, or cultural, reflect the influence of these opposing forces. Every challenge believers face bears the mark of a conflict that extends beyond the visible realm.

The aim of this book is to bring these enemies into clear focus, address them through sound biblical teaching, and present Christ as the definitive answer to their power.

With the reality of the battlefield established, we now begin where Scripture begins. We begin by tracing spiritual warfare from Genesis to Revelation, revealing the consistency of God's redemptive victory.

CHAPTER 1
SPIRITUAL WARFARE IN THE BIBLE: GENESIS TO REVELATION

This chapter fully develops the canonical framework introduced in the Introduction. Spiritual warfare is not an isolated doctrine or a marginal theme confined to select passages; it is a canonical reality that extends from Genesis to Revelation, revealing an ongoing conflict between the kingdom of God and the forces that oppose His rule and redemptive purposes. Biblical theologian G. K. Beale demonstrates that the scriptural narrative unfolds as a unified theological framework in which God's kingdom advances in the midst of cosmic opposition, culminating in its final consummation.[10] From the serpent in Eden to the dragon in the Apocalypse, Scripture consistently portrays this conflict as real, personal, and cosmic. As Richard Bauckham, in *The Theology of the Book of Revelation*, explains, the imagery of Revelation unveils this conflict as a theological drama in which divine sovereignty ultimately triumphs over all opposing powers.[11]

The Bible presents spiritual warfare not simply as human struggle but as conflict involving supernatural powers that operate behind historical events, moral decisions, and systems of false

---

[10] G. K. Beale, *A New Testament Biblical Theology* (Grand Rapids, MI: Baker Academic, 2011).

[11] Richard Bauckham, *The Theology of the Book of Revelation* (Cambridge: Cambridge University Press, 1993).

worship. Victory in this warfare is never achieved through human strength, political dominance, or mystical techniques, but through faith, obedience, and reliance upon God's sovereign power. Clinton E. Arnold, in *Powers of Darkness: Principalities and Powers in Paul's Letters*, emphasizes that spiritual warfare is fundamentally expressed through resistance to evil powers and the proclamation of the gospel."[12]

Eden as Sacred Space and the Origin of Conflict (Satan)

The Garden of Eden functions as more than an agricultural setting; it is a proto-temple, a sacred space in which God dwells with humanity. Adam is portrayed as a priestly figure charged with guarding and cultivating this holy domain (Genesis 2:15). Biblical theologian G. K. Beale, in *The Temple and the Church's Mission*, argues that Eden should be understood as an archetypal temple, with Adam functioning as a priestly guardian commissioned to preserve the sanctity of God's dwelling place.[13] Within this context, the entrance of the serpent represents more than temptation; it is an act of spiritual intrusion into the divine presence. Satan's deception constitutes an assault on divine order, aiming to corrupt worship, distort obedience, and sever communion between God and humanity (Genesis 3:1–6). As G. K. Beale demonstrates in *The Temple and the Church's Mission*, the biblical narrative unfolds as a sustained conflict between God's purpose to dwell with humanity and opposing forces that seek to resist and corrupt that purpose.[14]

---

[12] Clinton E. Arnold, *Powers of Darkness: Principalities and Powers in Paul's Letters* (Downers Grove, IL: InterVarsity Press, 1992).

[13] G. K. Beale, *The Temple and the Church's Mission: A Biblical Theology of the Dwelling Place of God* (Downers Grove, IL: InterVarsity Press, 2004).

[14] G. K. Beale, *The Temple and the Church's Mission: A Biblical Theology of the Dwelling Place of God* (Downers Grove, IL: InterVarsity Press, 2004),.

This episode lays the foundational pattern for Satan's activity throughout Scripture. He appears consistently as the adversary who seeks to defile sacred space, accuse God's people, and resist the advancement of God's kingdom (See Job 1–2; Zechariah 3:1–2; Revelation 12:9–10.) T. Desmond Alexander's analysis reinforces the biblical portrait of Satan as a real and personal enemy whose authority is derivative and temporary, operating only under divine permission.[15] As George Eldon Ladd argues in his theology of the kingdom, the kingdom of God is best understood as God's redemptive reign, inaugurated in the person and mission of Jesus Christ and awaiting its final consummation at the end of the age."[16]

Genesis: The War Begins in Eden (Genesis 3)

The first recorded act of spiritual warfare occurs in the garden of Eden when the serpent introduces deception by questioning the Word of God: "Did God really say…?"

Now the serpent was more crafty than any of the wild animals the Lord God had made. He said to the woman, "Did God really say, 'You must not eat from any tree in the garden'?"

The woman said to the serpent, "We may eat fruit from the trees in the garden, but God did say, 'You must not eat fruit from the tree that is in the middle of the garden, and you must not touch it, or you will die.'"

"You will not certainly die," the serpent said to the woman. "For God knows that when you eat from it your eyes will be opened, and you will be like God, knowing good and evil."

---

[15] T. Desmond Alexander, *From Eden to the New Jerusalem: An Introduction to Biblical Theology* (Grand Rapids, MI: Kregel, 2008), 98–105.

[16] George Eldon Ladd, *A Theology of the New Testament* (Grand Rapids: Eerdmans, 1993).

When the woman saw that the fruit of the tree was good for food and pleasing to the eye, and desirable for gaining wisdom, she took some and ate it. She also gave some to her husband, who was with her, and he ate it. Then the eyes of both were opened, and they realized they were naked; so, they sewed fig leaves together and made coverings for themselves (Genesis 3:1–7).

As Sinclair B. Ferguson explains in his discussion of Genesis 3, the serpent's temptation targets the authority of God's Word, calls into question the goodness of His character, and challenges humanity's identity as dependent creatures.[17]

Satan's plan is that deception precedes disobedience, and moral collapse is rooted in theological distortion. Eve's temptation unfolds through a deliberate triad. It was "good for food," "pleasing to the eye," and "desirable for gaining wisdom," a pattern that Scripture later shows as the framework of temptation (1 John 2:16).

"So, the Lord God said to the serpent, 'Because you have done this,

"Cursed are you above all livestock and all wild animals! You will crawl on your belly and you will eat dust all the days of your life. And I will put enmity between you and the woman, and between your offspring and hers; he will crush your head, and you will strike his heel.'" (Genesis 3:14–15)

Genesis 3:14–15 establishes both divine judgment and redemptive hope. God curses the serpent, announces ongoing enmity between the serpent and the woman's offspring, and promises a future descendant who will suffer injury yet crush the serpent's authority. This passage, commonly identified as the

---

[17] Sinclair B. Ferguson, *The Christian Life: A Doctrinal Introduction* (Edinburgh: Banner of Truth, 2015), 23–27.

protoevangelium, introduces the expectation of a messianic victory that finds its fulfillment in Jesus Christ.

Exodus to Kings: Deliverance and the War for Worship

Scripture presents Israel's conflicts as manifestations of a deeper spiritual war centered on exclusive worship. This is made explicit in the Exodus, where Yahweh declares judgment 'against all the gods of Egypt,' exposing Pharaoh as more than a political tyrant and as the representative of a false spiritual system. Through the plagues, God dismantles Egypt's religious worldview and reveals His absolute sovereignty over creation, life, death, and history. The plagues narrative of Exodus 7–12 functions as more than a record of miraculous deliverance and constitutes a sustained theological polemic against the religious system of Egypt. The text frames the events as divine judgment "against all the gods of Egypt" (Exodus 12:12). This indicates the plagues are directed confrontations with Egypt's cosmology, theology, and political ideology. Each plague confronts a domain associated with a specific Egyptian deity. Biblical theology understands these not as a simple statue, but as the manifestation of a real spiritual power that Yahweh exposes and judges. (In Scripture, idolatry is linked with demonic powers rather than neutral abstractions. See Deuteronomy 32:17; Psalm 106:37; 1 Corinthians 10:20).

The Nile, revered as the source of life and personified by deities such as Hapi and Khnum, becomes a vehicle of death. Fertility symbols associated with childbirth and abundance are transformed into instruments of affliction. The earth, sky, livestock, and human body, each under the supposed guardianship of various gods, fall under Yahweh's direct command. Even Pharaoh, regarded as the living embodiment of divine kingship, proves powerless, culminating in the death of the firstborn and the collapse of Egypt's royal theology.

The progressive intensity of the plagues reveals a deliberate movement: from public signs to cosmic disruption, and finally to judgment. Particularly significant is the plague of darkness, which confronts Ra, the supreme solar deity and ideological foundation of Pharaoh's authority. The climactic death of the firstborn exposes the impotence of Osiris, the god of resurrection, and publicly denies Egypt's claims to control life beyond death.

Crucially, the narrative emphasizes distinction. From the fourth plague onward, Yahweh differentiates between Egypt and Israel, underscoring covenantal election and divine sovereignty. Power is not arbitrary but purposeful, ordered toward redemption and revelation. The plagues thus serve a dual function: judgment upon false gods and self-disclosure of Yahweh as the sole, living God.

Within the broader realm of spiritual powers, Exodus presents a foundational paradigm. Salvation is achieved not only through liberation from physical bondage but through the overthrow of rival spiritual authorities. The Exodus affirms uncompromising monotheism: Yahweh does more than defeat other gods; He exposes them as devoid of real authority. History, nature, life, and death all answer to Him alone. See Table A.1 in the appendix.

This pattern continues throughout Israel's story. In the wilderness, Israel's greatest danger is not military defeat but idolatry. During the conquest and the period of the Judges, Israel's enemies succeeded primarily by drawing the nation into syncretism and divided allegiance.

Under the monarchy, foreign threats persist, yet national stability rises and falls with covenant faithfulness to Yahweh alone, while tolerated idolatry leads to collapse and exile. These developments reveal that Israel's enemies function as instruments within a broader spiritual conflict in which Satan seeks to destroy God's people by displacing Yahweh from His rightful place as their sole object of worship. This conflict unfolds from Genesis to the time of Christ, where Satan's opposition culminates to eliminate the Messiah, only to be decisively defeated through the cross. Across redemptive history, Israel's enemies serve as visible agents of an invisible war, yet at every stage, God demonstrates His sovereignty by transforming opposition into the means of redemption.

The canonical witness, therefore, confirms the central claim of *Know Your Enemies*: Spiritual warfare is fundamentally about worship. Land, power, and politics are secondary; the true conflict has always been over who one acknowledges as Lord, a conflict finally resolved in Christ's victory.

During the monarchy, David frames warfare as a matter of divine honor rather than human capability.

David said to the Philistine, "You come against me with sword and spear and javelin, but I come against you in the name of the Lord Almighty, the God of the armies of Israel, whom you have defied. This day the Lord will deliver you into my hands, and I will strike you down and cut off your head. This very day I will give the carcasses of the Philistine army to the birds and the wild animals, and the whole world will know that there is a God in Israel. All those gathered here will know that it is not by sword or spear that the Lord saves; *for the battle is the Lord's*, and he will give all of you into our hands." (1 Samuel 17:45–47).

In contrast, Saul and later kings experienced decline through disobedience and divided loyalty, culminating in Solomon's fall through syncretism and compromise (See 1 Kings 11:1–11).

These narratives establish a consistent biblical principle: Faith in the Lord and spiritual faithfulness secures victory, while divided worship invites defeat.

See Table A.2 in the appendix.

Alignment with Ephesians Chapter 6
The spiritual warfare depicted from Exodus to Kings anticipates the New Testament teaching of Ephesians 6:10–18. Israel's conflicts reveal the true struggle was never against human enemies alone but against spiritual rebellion expressed through idolatry, deception, fear, and disobedience, as seen in Deuteronomy 6:13–15 and Judges 2:12.

Deuteronomy 6:13–15 (ESV)

- **Fear and Serve the Lord:** "It is the Lord your God you shall fear. Him you shall serve and by his name you shall swear."

- **No Other Gods:** "You shall not go after other gods, the gods of the peoples who are around you."

- **Jealous God:** "For the Lord your God, who is among you, is a jealous God and his anger will burn against you, and he will destroy you from the face of the land."

Judges 2:12 (ESV)

- **Provoking the Jealousy of God:** "And they abandoned the

- Lord, the God of their fathers, who had brought them out of the land of Egypt. They went after other gods, from among the gods of the peoples who were around them, and bowed down to them. And they provoked the Lord to anger."

Paul later clarifies this reality by stating believers wrestle "not against flesh and blood, but against rulers, authorities, and spiritual forces of evil" (Ephesians 6:12). The Old Testament emphasis on obedience, faith, truth, and reliance on God (Exodus 14:13–14; Joshua 1:7–9; 1 Samuel 17:47) corresponds directly to the armor of God: truth, righteousness, faith, salvation, the Word of God, and prayer (Ephesians 6:13–18). Thus, Ephesians 6 does not introduce a new doctrine but, in Christ-centered terms, explains the same warfare Israel faced, one in which victory flows from exclusive loyalty to God and dependence on His power.

Job: Satan as Accuser and the Mystery of Permission
The narrative of Job advances the biblical portrayal of Satan by placing his activity within the heavenly court. In this setting, the adversary is neither independent nor equal to God but operates under divine authority and constraint. The text establishes a central theological tension: Satan acts with genuine hostility, yet only within limits determined by God. This tension frames both his role as accuser and the mystery of divine permission that governs his activity.

The scene opens with the "sons of God" presenting themselves before the Lord, indicating a formal assembly of the heavenly court. Satan appears among them not as a coequal power, but as the adversary whose function is investigative and accusatory. His report, "from roaming throughout the earth", suggests a continual observation of human conduct with the aim of exposing fault. The exchange that follows demonstrates that his activity is neither autonomous nor unrestricted, each action proceeds only under divine scrutiny and authorization. The narrative therefore establishes a critical theological principle: accusation operates within, not outside of, the sovereignty of God.

Satan as Accuser in the Heavenly Court

- **Job 1:6–7** "One day the angels came to present themselves before the Lord, and Satan also came with them. The Lord said to Satan, 'Where have you come from?' Satan answered the Lord, 'From roaming throughout the earth, going back and forth on it.'"

Old Testament scholar Carol A. Newsom explains that the Satan in the book of Job functions as an accuser within the divine council, challenging the integrity of human righteousness.[18] This scene establishes a judicial setting in which Satan appears before God to contest the authenticity of Job's righteousness, alleging that his obedience is transactional rather than genuine (Job 1:9–11).

- **Job 1:9–11** "Does Job fear God for no reason? Have you not put a hedge around him…? But stretch out your hand and touch all that he has, and he will curse you to your face."

Satan's Malice: Intent to Destroy Faith

- **Job 2:4–5** "Skin for skin! All that a man has he will give for his life. But stretch out your hand and touch his bone and his flesh, and he will curse you to your face."

Satan's objective is not suffering alone, but the destruction of Job's faith and integrity in order to provoke apostasy.

Satan's Limitation: Divine Permission and Boundaries

- **Job 1:12** "And the LORD said to Satan, 'Behold, all that he has is in your hand. Only against him do not stretch out your hand.'"

Satan is explicitly restricted by God's command.

---

[18] Carol A. Newsom, *The Book of Job: A Contest of Moral Imaginations* (Oxford: Oxford University Press, 2003).

- **Job 2:6** "And the LORD said to Satan, 'Behold, he is in your hand; only spare his life.'"

The book of Job makes clear that Satan's activity operates only within divinely imposed limits, demonstrating that all hostile powers remain subject to God's sovereign authority. (Job 2:6). While Satan functions as the immediate agent of affliction, God remains sovereign over both the scope and outcome of the conflict.

God's Sovereignty over the Conflict

- **Job 42:11** "They showed him sympathy… for all the evil that the LORD had brought upon him."

New Testament Parallels Confirming the Pattern
This pattern is confirmed later in Scripture. In Zechariah 3:1–2, Satan accuses Joshua the high priest, but the LORD rebukes him. In Luke 22:31–32, Satan demands to sift Peter, yet Christ's intercession preserves his faith.

- **Zechariah 3:1–2** Satan stands to accuse Joshua the high priest, but the LORD rebukes him.

- **Luke 22:31–32** "Simon, Simon, behold, Satan demanded to have you… but I have prayed for you."

In 1 Corinthians 10:13, God limits temptation, so it is never beyond endurance.

Psalms: Prayer and Worship as Spiritual Warfare
Walter Brueggemann emphasizes that the Psalms give voice to Israel's life before God, encompassing lament, trust, and praise as the community brings its needs, struggles, and hope for deliverance into the presence of God."[19] In the ongoing struggle against Satan and his forces, Christians have historically turned to

---

[19] Walter Brueggemann, *The Message of the Psalms* (Minneapolis: Augsburg, 1984).

the Psalms as a means of spiritual formation and engagement. Rather than promoting retaliation or hopelessness, these sacred songs shape the believer's response through prayerful dependence and honest lament. These songs help the believer's response through steadfast trust and worship.

The Psalms consistently testify that safety is not found in a conflict-free existence, but in communion with the ever-present God. Walter Brueggemann emphasizes that the Psalms portray life as a contested reality, in which prayer serves as a primary means by which God's people engage the tensions of faith"[20] Together with the work of Patrick D. Miller, the Psalms do not promise a life free from trouble; rather, they locate the worshipper within the sphere of God's sovereign care, giving voice to Israel's experience of conflict and teaching the faithful how to bring that struggle into the presence of God.[21]

Spiritual warfare means:

- **Satan's attacks are temporary**
- **God's presence is eternal**
- **The war ends in communion, not conflict**

Psalm 23 teaches that spiritual warfare is won not by aggression, but by submission to the Shepherd. The devil's strategies, fear, accusation, isolation, and exhaustion are neutralized by God's presence, provision, protection, and promise.

Psalm 23
The Lord is my shepherd, I lack nothing.

---

[20] Walter Brueggemann, *The Message of the Psalms* (Minneapolis: Augsburg, 1984).

[21] Patrick D. Miller, *Interpreting the Psalms* (Philadelphia: Fortress Press, 1986).

He makes me lie down in green pastures, he leads me beside quiet waters, he refreshes my soul.

He guides me along the right paths for his name's sake.

Even though I walk through the darkest valley, I will fear no evil, for you are with me; your rod and your staff, they comfort me.

You prepare a table before me in the presence of my enemies.

You anoint my head with oil; my cup overflows.

Surely your goodness and love will follow me all the days of my life, and I will dwell in the house of the Lord forever.

Psalm 23 reveals that victory in spiritual warfare flows from living under God's shepherding authority, where fear is defeated, the enemy is restrained, and the believer is sustained by divine presence and protection.

Psalm 35 is one of our models appeal to divine justice in this fight against the adversaries

Psalm 35
Contend, Lord, with those who contend with me; fight against those who fight against me.

Take up shield and armor; arise and come to my aid. Brandish spear and javelin against those who pursue me. Say to me, "I am your salvation." May those who seek my life be disgraced and put to shame may those who plot my ruin be turned back in dismay. May they be like chaff before the wind, with the angel of the Lord driving them away; may their path be dark and slippery, with the angel of the Lord pursuing them.

Since they hid their net for me without cause and without cause dug a pit for me, may ruin overtake them by surprise, may the net they hid entangle them, may they fall into the pit, to their ruin. Then my soul will rejoice in the Lord and delight in his salvation.

My whole being will exclaim, "Who is like you, Lord?

You rescue the poor from those too strong for them, the poor and needy from those who rob them." Ruthless witnesses come forward; they question me on things I know nothing about.

They repay me evil for good and leave me like one bereaved.

Yet when they were ill, I put on sackcloth and humbled myself with fasting.

When my prayers returned to me unanswered, I went about mourning as though for my friend or brother. I bowed my head in grief as though weeping for my mother.

But when I stumbled, they gathered in glee; assailants gathered against me without my knowledge. They slandered me without ceasing. Like the ungodly they maliciously mocked, they gnashed their teeth at me. How long, Lord, will you look on? Rescue me from their ravages, my precious life from these lions. I will give you thanks in the great assembly; among the throngs I will praise you. Do not let those gloat over me who are my enemies without cause; do not let those who hate me without reason maliciously wink the eye.

They do not speak peaceably, but devise false accusations against those who live quietly in the land. They sneer at me and say, "Aha! Aha! With our own eyes we have seen it."

Lord, you have seen this; do not be silent. Do not be far from me, Lord. Awake, and rise to my defense! Contend for me, my God and Lord. Vindicate me in your righteousness, Lord my God; do not let them gloat over me. Do not let them think, "Aha, just what we wanted!" or say, "We have swallowed him up." May all who gloat over my distress be put to shame and confusion; may all who exalt themselves over me be clothed with shame and disgrace. May those who delight in my vindication shout for joy and gladness; may they always say, "The Lord be exalted, who delights in the well-being of his servant." My tongue will proclaim your righteousness, your praises all day long.

This psalm portrays spiritual warfare as a cry for God's intervention against unjust and malicious enemies, teaching believers to entrust vindication to the LORD rather than seeking personal revenge. It reveals that when the righteous are falsely accused, pursued, or oppressed, God rises as defender, exposing deception, overturning evil schemes, and delivering His people. Therefore, He is affirming that victory in spiritual warfare comes through prayer, righteousness, and reliance on God's justice rather than human retaliation.

Psalm 91 emphasizes divine protection for those who dwell in God's presence.

Psalm 91

Whoever dwells in the shelter of the Most High will rest in the shadow of the Almighty.

I will say of the Lord, "He is my refuge and my fortress, my God, in whom I trust."

Surely he will save you from the fowler's snare and from the deadly pestilence.

He will cover you with his feathers, and under his wings you will find refuge; his faithfulness will be your shield and rampart.

You will not fear the terror of night, nor the arrow that flies by day, nor the pestilence that stalks in the darkness, nor the plague that destroys at midday.

A thousand may fall at your side, ten thousand at your right hand, but it will not come near you.

You will only observe with your eyes and see the punishment of the wicked.

If you say, "The Lord is my refuge," and you make the Most High your dwelling, no harm will overtake you, no disaster will come near your tent.

For he will command his angels concerning you to guard you in all your ways; they will lift you up in their hands, so that you will not strike your foot against a stone.

You will tread on the lion and the cobra; you will trample the great lion and the serpent.

"Because he loves me," says the Lord, "I will rescue him; I will protect him, for he acknowledges my name. He will call on me, and I will answer him; I will be with him in trouble, I will deliver him and honor him. With long life I will satisfy him and show him my salvation."

Psalm 91 presents spiritual warfare as life lived under God's protective authority, assuring believers that those who dwell in God's presence are shielded from the devil's attacks, fear, and destruction. It teaches that divine refuge, angelic protection, and trust in God's promises overcome Satan's threats, affirming that safety and victory in spiritual warfare flow from abiding in the LORD rather than from human strength or fear.

Together, the Psalms reveal that spiritual warfare is relational rather than aggressive and that victory flows from trust, submission, and worship.

Prophets: Pride, Tyranny, and the Cosmic Pattern
The prophetic literature exposes the spiritual forces and Satan the devil behind human pride and political tyranny. Isaiah 14 and Ezekiel 28, while addressing historical rulers, employ exalted language that reveals a deeper pattern of rebellion, self-exaltation, and judgment. These passages unveil the spiritual logic that energizes both satanic rebellion and human oppression.

Hell has been prepared by God for Satan, the fallen angels, and all who persist in rebellion against Him.

"For a Topheth is prepared of old; yea, for the king it is made ready; he hath made it deep and large: the pile thereof is fire and much wood; the breath of the LORD, like a stream of brimstone, doth kindle it." (Isaiah 30:33)

Cross-referenced Revelation 19:19–20; 20:14–15

"And I saw the beast, and the kings of the earth, and their armies, gathered together to make war against him that sat upon the horse, and against his army. And the beast was taken, and with him the false prophet that wrought the signs in his sight, wherewith he deceived them that had received the mark of the beast, and them that worshipped his image: they twain were cast alive into the lake of fire that burneth with brimstone." (Revelation 19:19–20)

Isaiah 30:33 presents Topheth as a place of judgment God prepared in advance, ignited not by human hands but by the very breath of the LORD, described as a stream of brimstone. While the immediate reference concerns judgment upon a rebellious earthly king, the text shows a broader biblical pattern in which hostile human rulers function as typological representatives of deeper spiritual rebellion. In this sense, the "king" anticipates the ultimate adversary, Satan himself, whose final judgment is revealed in Revelation as the lake of fire. Scripture consistently states that God prepared this place of judgment for the devil, his angels, and those who rebel against divine authority. This shows how prophetic warnings connect to future fulfillment.

Delayed Answered Prayer and Angelic Conflict (Danielic Foundation)

The reality of satanic hindrance is a reality. A foundational Old Testament witness appears in Daniel 10, where spiritual opposition explicitly delays the answer to prayer despite immediate divine response.

Daniel records that from the first day he set his heart to understand and to humble himself before God, his prayer was heard (Daniel 10:12). Yet the angelic messenger explains:

Then he continued, "Do not be afraid, Daniel. Since the first day that you set your mind to gain understanding and to humble yourself before your God, your words were heard, and I have come in response to them. But the prince of the Persian kingdom resisted me twenty-one days. Then Michael, one of the chief princes, came to help me, because I was detained there with the king of Persia. Now I have come to explain to you what will happen to your people in the future, for the vision concerns a time yet to come." (Daniel 10:12–14)

This passage reveals a critical truth: answered prayer may be delayed, not denied, due to real spiritual conflict in the unseen realm. The "prince of Persia" is not a human ruler but a territorial spiritual power, later opposed by Michael, described as *"one of the chief princes"* (Daniel 10:13).

Daniel's experience provides a precedent for Paul's later

theology of satanic hindrance. Just as Paul could say, *"Satan hindered us"* (1 Thessalonians 2:18), Daniel learns that spiritual resistance can obstruct divine communication and mission timing, without overturning God's will.

We should note that Daniel does not rebuke the demon, fast to manipulate God, or abandon prayer. Instead, he persists in humility, fasting, and faith, demonstrating that perseverance is itself an act of spiritual warfare. The delay magnifies the scope of the conflict and confirms that heaven had already responded.

Thus, Daniel 10 establishes three enduring warfare principles later assumed by Paul:

1 God responds immediately to genuine prayer.

2 Satanic powers can temporarily hinder the *delivery* of God's answer.

3 Persistent faith participates in unseen victory.

This Danielic framework illuminates Paul's lived experience of missionary obstruction, delayed travel, affliction, and resistance, all of which occur within a cosmic battlefield governed by God's sovereign authority.

Gospels, Epistles, and Revelation: Conflict and Resolution
The Gospels portray Jesus Christ as directly confronting the kingdom of darkness through temptation, exorcism, proclamation, and ultimately the cross (Matthew 4; John 12:31–32).

The Epistles instruct the church to engage in warfare through truth, holiness, endurance, and prayer rather than physical force (Ephesians 6; 2 Corinthians 10).

The book of Revelation concludes the biblical narrative by revealing the final defeat of Satan, the vindication of God's people, and the establishment of a new creation under Christ's eternal reign. "Woe to the earth and the sea, because the devil has gone down to you! He is filled with fury, because he knows that his time is short" (Revelation 12:12). As G. K. Beale demonstrates in The Book of Revelation, Satan's "great wrath" in Revelation 12:12 is best understood as the consequence of his expulsion from heaven and his recognition that his allotted time is short. Beale interprets this fury as inherently eschatological and fundamentally reactionary, not an expression of continued dominion but the response of a defeated adversary facing the certainty of impending judgment.[22]

With the canonical framework established, we now turn directly to the enemy himself, his origin, nature, authority, and limitations.

Having traced the biblical storyline of spiritual conflict, we now turn to Christ Himself, whose victory defines and governs all spiritual warfare.

---

[22] G. K. Beale, *The Book of Revelation*, New International Greek Testament Commentary (Grand Rapids: Eerdmans, 1999), 677.

CHAPTER 2
THE TEMPTATION OF CHRIST
VICTORY OVER SATAN IN THE WILDERNESS

One of the most critical passages for understanding spiritual warfare in the New Testament is the temptation of Jesus Christ in the wilderness. Immediately following His baptism, Jesus was led by the Spirit into the wilderness to be tempted by Satan (Matthew 4:1). This encounter is not merely a narrative detail in the gospel account. Rather, it is a theological battleground in which the authority of God's Word, the nature of temptation, and Satan's defeat are clearly revealed.

Matthew chapter 4 presents Christ not as a passive victim of temptation, but as the obedient Son who triumphs where all others have failed. In this confrontation, Jesus stands as the Second Adam and the true Israel, overcoming Satan through unwavering submission to the will and Word of God.

The Divine Purpose of the Temptation

Jesus's temptation was neither accidental nor a sign of moral weakness. Scripture is explicit that Jesus was without sin, yet fully capable of experiencing temptation (Hebrews 4:15). The Holy Spirit led Jesus into the wilderness, underscoring that this encounter was permitted and governed by God's sovereign purpose (Matthew 4:1). Several theological purposes are evident:

1 **To affirm Christ's true humanity:** Jesus experienced genuine hunger, isolation, and weakness after fasting forty days and forty nights (Matthew 4:2). His obedience was not theoretical but tested under real human conditions.

2 **To reveal Jesus as the Second Adam**: Where Adam fell in a garden surrounded by abundance, Jesus triumphed in a wilderness marked by deprivation (Romans 5:18 19).

3 **To demonstrate victory over Satan at the outset of His ministry**: Before casting out demons publicly, Jesus defeats Satan privately through obedience.

4 **To model spiritual resistance for believers:** Jesus's responses provide a pattern for confronting temptation through Scripture, submission, and faith.

The First Temptation: Appetite and Independence from God (Matthew 4:3–4)

After forty days of fasting, Satan approached Jesus with the words, "If you are the Son of God, tell these stones to become bread." This temptation targeted Jesus's physical hunger but carried a deeper spiritual aim to entice Him to act independently of the Father's will.

Jesus responded by quoting Deuteronomy 8:3: "Man shall not live on bread alone, but on every word that comes from the mouth of God."

This response reveals that the temptation was not about food, but about authority and trust. Satan sought to undermine Jesus's dependence on God by encouraging Him to use divine power for self-gratification rather than obedience. Some theological reflection of this:

- Legitimate needs can become illegitimate temptations when satisfied outside God's will.

- Victory over temptation begins with submission to God's Word rather than reliance on circumstances or power.

The Second Temptation: Presumption and Testing God (Matthew 4:5–7)
Satan next took Jesus to the pinnacle of the temple and urged Him to throw Himself down, citing Psalm 91 as proof of divine protection. This temptation was subtle, cloaked in Scripture, and aimed at provoking Jesus to demand a public sign from God.

Jesus replied with Deuteronomy 6:16: "Do not put the Lord your God to the test."

Here, Satan misused Scripture by divorcing it from obedience and humility. Jesus exposed this distortion by affirming that faith does not manipulate God or demand proof of His faithfulness. Now, some conceptual clarity of this is:

1 **Satan often uses Scripture deceptively.**
2 **True faith trusts the promises of God without forcing**
3 **His hand.**
4 **Obedience rejects spectacle in favor of submission.**

The Third Temptation: Worship and Authority Without the Cross (Matthew 4:8–10)
In the final temptation, Satan offered Jesus all the kingdoms of the world in exchange for worship. This was a direct assault on Christ's mission, offering glory without suffering and authority

without obedience.

Jesus responded decisively: "Worship the Lord your God, and serve him only" (Deuteronomy 6:13; Matthew 4:10).

This temptation struck at the heart of worship and allegiance. Satan sought to divert Jesus from the path of suffering obedience that would lead to the cross. For this one, we see:

1 **Satan offers shortcuts that bypass God's redemptive plan.**

2 **Worship belongs exclusively to God.**

3 **Christ chose the cross before the crown.**

The Defeat of Satan and the Ministry of Angels (Matthew 4:11)
After resisting all three temptations, Jesus commanded Satan to leave. The devil departed, and angels came to minister to Him. This moment marks a decisive defeat of Satan and affirms Christ's authority.

Though Satan would continue to oppose Jesus throughout His ministry, the outcome was already assured. Christ's obedience in the wilderness foreshadowed His ultimate victory at the cross and resurrection.

Christological and Warfare Implications
The temptation narrative reveals several enduring truths:

1 **Jesus is the victorious Son of God.**

2 **Scripture is the believer's primary weapon in spiritual warfare (Ephesians 6:17).**

3 **Satan is real but limited, operating under God's sovereignty.**

4 **Victory comes through obedience, not power displays.**

5   Jesus did not overcome Satan by miracles, but by faithfulness to God's Word, demonstrating that believers, empowered by the Spirit, can also resist the devil (James 4:7).

Matthew chapter 4 presents Christ as the triumphant Messiah who confronted Satan and emerged victorious through obedience, humility, and unwavering trust in God's Word. His victory in the wilderness establishes the pattern for Christian resistance against temptation and confirms Satan's ultimate defeat.

As believers engage in spiritual warfare today, they do so not from a position of fear, but from victory, secured by Christ, demonstrated in the wilderness, and consummated at the cross and resurrection.

Christ's triumph over Satan in the wilderness presupposes the reality of a personal adversary, whose origin, nature, and limitations must now be examined.

CHAPTER 3

SATAN—THE DEVIL
THE EXTERNAL SPIRITUAL ENEMY

The Origin, Nature, and Limitations of Satan

The Bible presents Satan as a real, personal, intelligent, and malevolent spiritual being who stands in deliberate opposition to God and His redemptive purposes. Scripture does not portray Satan as an abstract symbol of evil or a mythological construct, but as a created being whose activity unfolds within God's sovereign rule.

Throughout this work, Greek terms are cited to clarify theological meaning rather than to engage in a technical linguistic approach. The term *Satan* derives from the Hebrew *śāṭān*, meaning "adversary" or "accuser," emphasizing hostility, opposition, and legal indictment. In the Greek New Testament, Σατανᾶς (Satanas) identifies the enemy primarily by his *oppositional stance* against God's redemptive purposes, while διάβολος (diábolos) highlights his *method*, deception, accusation, and slander.[23] Together, these terms present Satan not as an abstract force, but as a personal, intelligent adversary whose power is real, yet subordinate and whose defeat is secured through Christ.

Satan was originally created as a great angel, perfect and good,

---

[23] (See *Greek–English Lexicon of the New Testament and Other Early Christian Literature*, 3rd ed., entries for "Satan" and "devil"; HALOT, entry for "Satan"; TDOT, vol. 14; TDNT, vol. 2.)

and was appointed to serve in a ministerial capacity before the throne of God. However, at some point before the creation of the world, he rebelled against God and thus became the principal adversary of both God and humanity (Ezekiel 28:12–15). In his rebellion, Satan drew after himself a vast number of lesser angels, who fell with him and are subsequently identified as demons or evil spirits (Revelation 12:4).

As a result of this rebellion, Satan and many of these fallen angels were cast down to the earth and the surrounding atmospheric realm, where they continue to operate under the permissive will and sovereign authority of God. Though active, their power is neither autonomous nor absolute.

Satan, also referred to in Scripture as "the serpent," was instrumental in bringing about the fall of humanity through deception and temptation in the garden of Eden (Genesis 3:1–6). His dominion constitutes a highly organized and structured kingdom of evil, exercising influence and authority over several spheres:

- the lower heavenly or atmospheric realm (Ephesians 2:2),

- fallen angels under his command (Matthew 25:41;

- Revelation 12:7), unregenerate humanity, who remain under his influence apart from Christ (John 12:31; Ephesians 2:2), and

- the present world system, which he seeks to control and corrupt (Luke 4:5–6; 2 Corinthians 4:4).

Despite his vast influence, Satan is neither omnipotent, omniscient, nor omnipresent. As a finite created being, he relies heavily on the delegation of authority and activity to demons to advance his purposes throughout the world.

Scripture rejects dualism. Satan is not equal to God in power, authority, or eternity. He is created, finite, accountable, fallen, and judged. Because Satan is created, he is limited. Because he is fallen, he is corrupt. Because he is judged, his defeat is certain.

Satan as a Created Being

Scripture consistently affirms that Satan is a created angelic being rather than an eternal or autonomous force. Passages such as Ezekiel 28 and Isaiah 14, when read typologically and canonically, indicate that Satan originally occupied a position of extraordinary privilege and authority within the heavenly order.

Isaiah 14:12–17

How you have fallen from heaven, morning star, son of the dawn!

You have been cast down to the earth, you who once laid low the nations!

You said in your heart, "I will ascend to the heavens; I will raise my throne above the stars of God; I will sit enthroned on the mount of assembly, on the utmost heights of Mount Zaphon. I will ascend above the tops of the clouds; I will make myself like the Most High."

But you are brought down to the realm of the dead, to the depths of the pit.

Those who see you stare at you, they ponder your fate: "Is this the man who shook the earth and made kingdoms tremble, the man who made the world a wilderness, who overthrew its cities and would not let his captives go home?"

Isaiah 14:12–17 depicts the dramatic fall of a proud ruler whose ambition to exalt himself above God leads to total humiliation and judgment. Jesus's statement in Luke 10:18, "I saw Satan fall like lightning from heaven," confirms and clarifies this pattern, revealing the fall described in Isaiah represents a real, decisive defeat of Satan's authority, not a purely poetic or historical reference. Using elevated and cosmic language, the passage exposes the inner logic of rebellion, self-deification, arrogance, and refusal to submit to God's sovereignty, and shows how such pride results in irreversible downfall. The text, originally targeting the Babylonian king, is now seen as revealing Satan's rebellion. It shows how God humbles both satanic and human powers that aim for divine status. The passage ultimately affirms that no power, earthly or spiritual, can usurp God's throne without facing decisive judgment. Satan's rebellion stands ultimately in direct contrast to the humility and obedience of Jesus Christ. While the passage exposes the pride-driven ambition behind satanic and human tyranny, its full meaning is clarified considering Christ, who did not grasp at equality with God but humbled Himself in obedience unto death (Philippians 2:6–8).

See Table A.3 in the appendix.

Ezekiel 28:11–19

The word of the Lord came to me: "Son of man, take up a lament concerning the king of Tyre and say to him: 'This is what the Sovereign Lord says: "You were the seal of perfection, full of wisdom and perfect in beauty. You were in Eden, the garden of God; every precious stone adorned you: carnelian, chrysolite and emerald, topaz, onyx and jasper, lapis lazuli, turquoise and beryl. Your settings and mountings were made of gold; on the day you were created they were prepared. You were anointed as a guardian cherub, for so I ordained you. You were on the holy mount of God; you walked among the fiery stones. You were blameless in your ways from the day you were created till wickedness was found in you. Through your widespread trade you were filled with violence, and you sinned. So I drove you in disgrace from the mount of God, and I expelled you, guardian cherub, from among the fiery stones. Your heart became proud on account of your beauty, and you corrupted your wisdom because of your splendor. So I threw you to the earth; I made a spectacle of you before kings. By your many sins and dishonest trade you have desecrated your sanctuaries. So I made a fire come out from you, and it consumed you, and I reduced you to ashes on the ground in the sight of all who were watching. All the nations who knew you are appalled at you; you have come to a horrible end and will be no more."'"

Ezekiel 28:11–19 is a prophetic lament that, while historically directed toward the king of Tyre, deliberately transcends any human ruler and unveils the pattern of *Satan's original glory and catastrophic fall.* The passage describes a being created in perfection, endowed with wisdom and extraordinary beauty, dwelling in Eden and identified as an "anointed guardian cherub" who occupied a privileged position in God's holy presence. This exalted status underscores that Satan was a created angelic being, not a rival deity, entrusted with authority and proximity to God.

The text traces Satan's fall to *pride and self-corruption,* as his heart became lifted because of his splendor, and his wisdom was perverted by self-exaltation. What began as divine stewardship degenerated into violence, deception, and defilement, leading to his expulsion from God's mountain and removal from his role as guardian. God's judgment is portrayed as both decisive and humiliating: Satan is cast down, exposed before kings, and ultimately reduced to ruin, serving as a warning to all who would exalt themselves against God.

Ezekiel 28 reveals Satan's rebellion started internally rather than externally, that his authority was delegated and therefore revocable, and that his judgment is certain and irreversible. The passage affirms God's absolute sovereignty over all spiritual beings and anticipates Satan's final destruction, while also exposing pride as the foundational sin behind both cosmic rebellion and earthly tyranny.

As Wayne Grudem argues in chapter 20 of *Systematic Theology*, Satan, as a created being, possesses genuine power and intelligence, yet these attributes are necessarily finite. Accordingly, he is powerful but not omnipotent, knowledgeable but not omniscient, and active within the created order but not omnipotent, knowledgeable but not omniscient, and active but not omnipresent.[24] These limitations are essential for sound spiritual warfare, guarding believers against fear-driven exaggeration on one hand and naïve dismissal on the other.

Ezekiel 10—The Cherubim and the Glory of God

Ezekiel 10 provides an essential context for understanding the cherubic imagery of Ezekiel 28. The chapter depicts cherubim as guardians of sacred space and bearers of the divine glory. The vision records the gradual departure of the glory of the LORD from the temple, a movement prompted by Israel's persistent idolatry and covenant violation.

This progressive withdrawal underscores the holiness of God and the seriousness of defilement within sacred space. The cherubim's proximity to the divine throne clarifies that the figure described in Ezekiel 28 originally occupied a position of immense trust and responsibility within the heavenly order.

Thus, Ezekiel 10 strengthens the typological reading of Ezekiel 28 by placing cherubic rebellion within a broader concept of

---

[24] Wayne Grudem, *Systematic Theology: An Introduction to Biblical Doctrine* (Grand Rapids: Zondervan, 1994), chap. 20.

holiness, sacred space, and divine presence.

The Reality and Personality of Satan

Modern theology often errs in one of two directions: denying Satan's personal existence or exaggerating his influence by attributing every struggle directly to demonic activity. Both errors distort biblical teaching and undermine spiritual discernment.

Scripture presents Satan as possessing intellect, will, desire, and intentional hostility toward God's people. The Scriptures describe Satan as a being who can speak in Genesis 3:1–5, accuse in Job 1–2, tempt in Matthew 4:1–11, deceive in Revelation 12:9, and seek to devour in 1 Peter 5:8. These actions cannot be reduced to impersonal forces or psychological abstractions. They are the reality of the person of Satan.

Satan's Authority Is Real but Limited

The Bible acknowledges Satan exercises real influence within the present world order, yet always within divinely imposed boundaries. In Job 1–2, Satan is permitted to test Job but is explicitly restricted by God regarding the extent of his actions. This narrative demonstrates Satan's power is derivative, not autonomous.

The New Testament reinforces this limitation. Satan cannot override human will, nullify God's promises, or separate believers from Christ (Romans 8:38–39). Even when Satan acts maliciously, God sovereignly governs the outcome, often using trials to refine faith rather than destroy it.

Understanding who Satan is prepares us to examine how he operates within redemptive history.

CHAPTER 4
DEMONS AND THEIR ROLE IN SPIRITUAL CONFLICT

This section expounds the biblical doctrine of Christ's authority over Satan and demons, drawing primarily from Mark 3:27 and the broader New Testament witness. It establishes the foundation for understanding spiritual warfare as Christ-centered, redemptive, and governed by divine sovereignty.

Scriptural Foundation of the Demons
Mark 3:27 declares: "No one can enter a strong man's house without first tying him up. Then he can plunder the strong man's house." This statement reveals Jesus's mission to confront, bind, and ultimately defeat Satan, liberating those held captive by demonic oppression.

The New Testament consistently acknowledges demonic activity as a central element of the spiritual conflict between the kingdoms of God and of Satan. Scripture frequently describes people who suffer under satanic oppression through the indwelling or influence of unclean spirits, and it records many confrontations between Jesus Christ and demonic forces. The gospel of Mark, particularly, presents repeated accounts of such encounters, demonstrating both the pervasiveness of demonic affliction and the unrivaled authority of Christ over evil spirits (Mark 5:1–20; 7:24–30; 9:14–29).

Mark 1:23–28 describes Jesus's first recorded exorcism in the synagogue at Capernaum, where a man with an unclean spirit recognizes Jesus as the Holy One of God. But Jesus silences and commands the spirit to leave the man; the event astonishes the crowd, who marvel at Jesus's new teaching and authority, causing His fame to spread rapidly throughout Galilee.

Just then a man in their synagogue who was possessed by an impure spirit cried out, "What do you want with us, Jesus of Nazareth? Have you come to destroy us? I know who you are, the Holy One of God!"

"Be quiet!" said Jesus sternly. "Come out of him!" The impure spirit shook the man violently and came out of him with a shriek.

The people were all so amazed that they asked each other, "What is this? A new teaching, and with authority! He even gives orders to impure spirits and they obey him." News about him spread quickly over the whole region of Galilee. (Mark 1:23–28)

Jesus Healed Many and Cast Out Demons
- That evening after sunset the people brought to Jesus all the sick and demon-possessed. The whole town gathered at the door, and Jesus healed many who had various diseases. He also drove out many demons, but he would not let the demons speak because they knew who he was. (Mark 1:32–34)

- For he had healed many, so that those with diseases were pushing forward to touch him. Whenever the impure spirits saw him, they fell down before him and cried out, "You are the Son of God." But he gave them strict orders not to tell others about him. (Mark 3:10–12)

Jesus Honors a Syrophoenician Woman's Faith, and Casts Out an Impure Spirit

Jesus left that place and went to the vicinity of Tyre. He entered a house and did not want anyone to know it; yet he could not keep his presence secret. In fact, as soon as she heard about him, a woman whose little daughter was possessed by an impure spirit came and fell at his feet. The woman was a Greek, born in Syrian Phoenicia. She begged Jesus to drive the demon out of her daughter.

"First let the children eat all they want," he told her, "for it is not right to take the children's bread and toss it to the dogs."

"Lord," she replied, "even the dogs under the table eat the children's crumbs."

Then he told her, "For such a reply, you may go; the demon has left your daughter."

She went home and found her child lying on the bed, and the demon gone." (Mark 7:24–30)

These narratives affirm that demonic power is real, personal, and active, yet decisively subordinate to the authority of the Son of God (Mark 1:27; Luke 10:17).

Demons are not abstract forces or impersonal energies. They are spirit beings possessing intelligence, will, and personal agency. As members of Satan's dominion, they stand in deliberate opposition to God and hostility toward humanity. Scripture portrays them as morally corrupt, malicious in intent, and operating under the authority of Satan himself (Matthew 12:43–45). Their activity reflects the nature of the kingdom they serve; one characterized by deception, destruction, and rebellion against divine order (John 8:44; 10:10).

Demons and Idols

The Bible further reveals that demonic influence lies behind idolatry and statues. The so-called gods of the nations are not neutral cultural symbols but are animated by demonic powers. Therefore, the worship of false gods is participation in demonic allegiance rather than mere religious error (1 Corinthians 10:20). Idolatry is not only a theological deviation but a spiritual submission that aligns human worship with forces opposed to the living God.

Demonic Powers and Unbelievers

In the New Testament worldview, the present world system is shown as alienated from God and under Satan's influence. "Now is the time for judgment on this world; now the prince of this world will be driven out" (John 12:31).

"The god of this age has blinded the minds of unbelievers, so that they cannot see the light of the gospel that displays the glory of Christ, who is the image of God" (2 Corinthians 4:4). According to 2 Corinthians 4:4, Satan, referred to as "the god of this age," exercises a blinding influence over the minds of unbelievers, obstructing their ability to recognize the light of the gospel that displays the glory of Christ, who embodies the image of God. The text highlights the reality of spiritual opposition, showing how the devil's deception functions to obscure divine truth and impede saving understanding.

Demonic powers are described as rulers and authorities operating within this fallen age, exercising influence over cultural, moral, and spiritual structures (Ephesians 6:10–12). For this reason, the Christian life is framed as ongoing spiritual warfare. Believers are not called to passive coexistence with evil but to vigilant resistance, standing firm against spiritual forces that seek to undermine faith, obedience, and truth (Ephesians 6:13; James 4:7).

Scripture also teaches that demons can inhabit human beings, particularly unbelievers, and frequently use their voices to speak through those they control (Mark 5:15; Acts 16:18).

As an example, Jesus restores a demon-possessed man, who recognized Jesus as the *"Most High God,"* and using the voice of the man to speak (Luke 8:26–39).

They sailed to the region of the Gerasene which is across the lake from Galilee. When Jesus stepped ashore, he was met by a demon-possessed man from the town. For a long time, this man had not worn clothes or lived in a house, but had lived in the tombs. When he saw Jesus, he cried out and fell at his feet, shouting at the top of his voice, "What do you want with me, Jesus, Son of the Most High God? I beg you, don't torture me!" For Jesus had commanded the impure spirit to come out of the man. Many times it had seized him, and though he was chained hand and foot and kept under guard, he had broken his chains and had been driven by the demon into solitary places.

Jesus asked him, "What is your name?"

"Legion," he replied, because many demons had gone into him. And they begged Jesus repeatedly not to order them to go into the Abyss.

A large herd of pigs was feeding there on the hillside. The demons begged Jesus to let them go into the pigs, and he gave them permission. When the demons came out of the man, they went into the pigs, and the herd rushed down the steep bank into the lake and was drowned.

When those tending the pigs saw what had happened, they ran off and reported this in the town and countryside, and the people went out to see what had happened. When they came to Jesus, they found the man from whom the demons had gone out, sitting at Jesus's feet, dressed and in his right mind; and they were afraid. Those who had seen it told the people how the demon-possessed man had been cured. Then all the people of the region of the Gerasenes asked Jesus to leave them, because they were overcome with fear. So he got into the boat and left.

The man from whom the demons had gone out begged to go with him, but Jesus sent him away, saying, "Return home and tell how much God has done for you." So, the man went away and told all over town how much Jesus had done for him.

Such possession results in severe bondage, distorting the will and leading individuals toward sin, immorality, and self-destruction. "Even while the boy was coming, the demon threw him to the ground in a convulsion. But Jesus rebuked the impure spirit, healed the boy and gave him back to his father" (Luke 9:42).

Demonic domination strips persons of freedom and dignity, emphasizing humanity's need for divine deliverance rather than self-reformation.

In some instances, demonic activity manifests through physical affliction, including muteness, blindness, seizures, and chronic infirmities (Matthew 9:32–33; 12:22; 17:14–18; Luke 13:11, 16). However, the New Testament carefully distinguishes between illness caused by evil spirits and sickness arising from natural causes (Matthew 4:24; Luke 5:12–13). Not all diseases result from demonic influence, and Scripture avoids simplistic explanations that attribute every form of suffering to spiritual possession. This balanced biblical perspective guards against both denial and exaggeration of demonic involvement in human suffering.

Engagement In Occultism

Engagement in occult practices, such as spiritism, divination, and sorcery, constitutes direct interaction with evil spirits and often results in deep spiritual bondage (Acts 13:8–10; 19:19; Galatians 5:20). Such practices open individuals to demonic control by seeking power, knowledge, or guidance apart from God. The New Testament consistently condemns these activities, warning they enslave rather than enlighten and ultimately lead to spiritual ruin (Revelation 9:20).

Demonic Activities in the Last Days

Finally, Scripture warns that demonic activity will intensify in the last days of this age. Evil spirits will promote deception, false religion, moral corruption, violence, and hostility toward divine truth (Matthew 24:24; 1 Timothy 4:1). They will actively oppose sound doctrine and seek to counterfeit God's work through false signs and wonders (2 Corinthians 11:14–15). The culmination of this demonic activity will be expressed through the Antichrist and those who align themselves with his rebellion (2 Thessalonians 2:9; Revelation 13:2–8; 16:13–14). Yet even in this final escalation of evil, Scripture affirms that demonic power remains temporary and destined for judgment under the ultimate victory of Christ (Colossians 2:15; Revelation 20:1–3, 10).

Remember that hell (Gehenna, the Sheol) was prepared for Satan and his demons, affirming their ultimate judgment and defeat (Matthew 25:41).

Believers and Spiritual Warfare

Scripture affirms that believers indwelt by the Holy Spirit cannot be demon-possessed, as light and darkness cannot coexist within the same temple (2 Corinthians 6:15–16). However, believers may experience demonic influence when they fail to walk in obedience and spiritual discernment.

2 Corinthians 6:15–16: "What harmony is there between Christ and Belial? Or what does a believer have in common with an unbeliever? What agreement is there between the temple of God and idols? For we are the temple of the living God. As God has said:

'I will live with them and walk among them and I will be their God, and they will be my people.'"

In 2 Corinthians 6:15–16, Paul employs antithetical pairings to underscore the irreconcilable divide between righteousness and lawlessness, Christ and Belial, faith and unbelief. He grounds this contrast in temple theology, declaring that believers are God's sanctuary, the sphere of His indwelling presence and covenant fellowship. The passage calls Christians to embodied holiness, urging separation from idolatrous influences, considering their identity as God's consecrated people.

Authority and Responsibility of Believers

Believers are granted authority in Christ to resist and overcome demonic forces (Luke 10:19). Spiritual warfare involves recognizing the true enemy, living a holy and obedient life, proclaiming the gospel, exercising faith, using the Word of God, prayer, fasting, and relying fully on the Holy Spirit.

This warfare is not against flesh and blood but against spiritual forces of evil in the heavenly realms (Ephesians 6:12). Victory is maintained through steadfast faith, truth, righteousness, and the power of Christ's name.

This chapter supports the book's central thesis:

1 Satan is a real, personal enemy defeated by Christ.

2 Demons operate within Satan's limited authority.

3 Christ's victory is final and absolute.

4 Believers engage in warfare from victory, not for victory.

5 The Word of God and the Holy Spirit are the believer's primary weapons.

Knowing the enemy begins with knowing Christ. Only through union with Him can believers stand firm, resist deception, and walk in spiritual freedom.

CHAPTER 5

SATAN'S STRATEGY IN REDEMPTIVE HISTORY

Knowing Christ is not only the foundation of resistance but the interpretive center through which the entire conflict must be understood. Union with Him secures the believer's position, yet it also unveils the deeper structure of opposition that unfolds across redemptive history. Satan's activity is neither episodic nor disordered; it follows a discernible pattern that corresponds to the advancing purposes of God. This pattern emerges progressively within the canon, anticipated in the prophetic visions of Daniel, intensified in the direct confrontation with Christ in the Gospels, and brought to full disclosure in the apocalyptic unveiling of Revelation. To grasp the present reality of spiritual conflict, one must therefore trace this developing strategy as it moves toward its appointed end.

The Consistency of Satanic Strategy

While Satan's methods adapt to historical and cultural contexts, Scripture reveals a consistent pattern in his strategies. His primary tactics are deception, accusation, and destruction. These strategies do not terminate in moral failure alone but aim at undermining trust in God's character and the authority of His Word. The assault is therefore theological at its core, targeting the foundation of belief before manifesting in conduct. As C. S. Lewis observes in *The*

Screwtape Letters (Letter XII), "the safest road to Hell is the gradual one, the gentle slope, soft underfoot, without sudden turnings, without milestones, without signposts."[25]

Deception as Primary Warfare (Genesis 3)

Satan's first recorded act is deception. By questioning God's Word, "Did God really say…?", he introduces doubt regarding divine revelation and authority. This moment establishes a foundational pattern in redemptive history: doctrinal distortion precedes moral collapse. The erosion of truth is the precondition for the corruption of conduct.

Deception rarely presents itself in overtly evil forms. It is often subtle, plausible, and persuasive, cloaked in partial truth and appealing reasoning. Scripture consistently warns that false teaching, half-truths, and doctrinal distortion constitute some of Satan's most effective instruments against the people of God. Through these means, he reshapes truth itself, leading individuals to embrace error under the appearance of legitimacy.

Accusation and Condemnation

Satan is identified as "the accuser of the brethren" (Revelation 12:10), seeking to produce shame, despair, and spiritual paralysis. His accusations function by distorting the believer's standing before God, shifting the focus from divine grace to perceived failure. The objective is not repentance, but disorientation and withdrawal from communion with God.

A critical distinction must therefore be maintained between accusation and conviction. Conviction is the work of the Holy Spirit, leading to repentance, restoration, and renewed fellowship. Accusation, by contrast, leads to hopelessness, self-condemnation, and distance from God.

---

[25] C. S. Lewis, *The Screwtape Letters* (New York: HarperOne, 2001), Letter XII.

The gospel provides the definitive answer to satanic accusation. Christ stands as Advocate and Intercessor for believers, ensuring that no charge can ultimately stand against those who are justified by faith (Romans 8:33–34; 1 John 2:1). The courtroom in which accusation is raised is the very place where it is decisively overturned through the finished work of Christ.

The Roaring Lion: Vigilance and Resistance (1 Peter 5:8–9)

The apostle Peter exhorts believers to sobriety and vigilance on the basis of a present and active threat: "Your adversary the devil prowls around like a roaring lion, seeking someone to devour" (1 Peter 5:8). This imagery presents Satan not as sovereign, but as a predatory and intentional adversary who operates with calculated opportunism. His activity is directed toward exploiting conditions of vulnerability, especially suffering and fear, in order to distort faith and undermine trust in God. As Peter H. Davids observes in his commentary on 1 Peter, the depiction of the devil as a roaring lion (1 Peter 5:8) echoes Psalm 22:13, where hostile forces are portrayed as predatory lions surrounding the righteous sufferer. This intertextual connection situates the believer's experience within the broader biblical pattern of righteous suffering under threat.[26]

This perspective is reinforced by theologian John Piper, who emphasizes that Satan operates within the bounds of divine providence. His strategies do not overturn God's sovereignty, but function through the manipulation of human weakness, seeking destructive ends through fear, discouragement, and disorientation.[27] The threat, therefore, lies not in autonomous

---

[26] Peter H. Davids, *The First Epistle of Peter*, New International Commentary on the New Testament (Grand Rapids: Eerdmans, 1990), 200.

[27] John Piper, *Job: When the Righteous Suffer* (Wheaton, IL: Crossway, 2012), 45–50.

power, but in calculated opposition that exploits real conditions within the fallen world.

The designation of Satan as a "roaring lion" (1 Peter 5:8) further intensifies the imagery. Peter H. Davids observes that this description echoes Psalm 22:13, where hostile forces are depicted as predatory lions surrounding the righteous sufferer, thereby situating the believer's experience within a broader biblical pattern of righteous suffering under threat.[28] The metaphor conveys intimidation, aggression, and the constant presence of danger. Yet the emphasis is not on ultimate power, but on the psychological and spiritual pressure exerted upon the believer. The roar is intended to instill fear, magnify perceived threat, and provoke instability in faith.

Within this framework, resistance is commanded, but its nature is carefully defined. Believers are instructed to resist "firm in the faith" (1 Peter 5:9), indicating that the primary mode of opposition is not aggressive confrontation, but steadfast trust in the truth of the gospel. Vigilance, therefore, is not a posture of fear or paranoia, but one of disciplined spiritual awareness rooted in confidence in God's sovereignty.

Names and Modes of Operation

Satan's strategies are further clarified by the names Scripture assigns to him, each revealing a distinct mode of operation. As "the devil" (διάβολος), he is the slanderer who distorts truth and maligns both God and His people. As "Satan" (Σατανᾶς), he is the adversary who opposes the purposes of God. As "the tempter" (Matthew 4:3), he entices toward disobedience. As "the deceiver of the whole world" (Revelation 12:9), he propagates falsehood on a global scale.

---

[28] Peter H. Davids, *The First Epistle of Peter*, New International Commentary on the New Testament (Grand Rapids, MI: Eerdmans, 1990), 189

These designations do not represent isolated functions, but interrelated expressions of a unified strategy. Deception leads to temptation, temptation gives rise to sin, and sin becomes the ground of accusation. In this way, Satan's activity operates as a coordinated system aimed at disrupting faith, corrupting truth, and opposing the redemptive purposes of God.

The Cross as Cosmic Defeat

The decisive defeat of Satan occurs at the cross. Colossians 2:15 declares that Christ "disarmed the powers and authorities" and triumphed over them publicly. In this act, the legal basis of Satan's accusations is nullified through the full satisfaction of divine justice.

Although Satan remains active until the final judgment, his authority is decisively broken. The strategies of deception, accusation, and intimidation persist, but they operate within the limits of a defeated adversary. Believers therefore engage in spiritual warfare not to achieve victory, but to stand in the victory already secured by Christ.

The conflict remains real, but its outcome is no longer uncertain.

CHAPTER 6

THE NAMES AND OPERATIONS OF SATAN IN SCRIPTURE

Biblical Nomenclature Reveals Satan's Activity and Strategy
Scripture reveals Satan through a wide range of names and titles rather than a single designation. This diversity of nomenclature is not ornamental but functional. Each name discloses a specific aspect of Satan's character, methods, authority, and objectives. Biblical nomenclature, therefore, functions as a theological diagnosis, equipping believers to discern how the enemy operates, how his work intersects with the flesh and the world, and how his strategies are decisively countered by the finished work of Christ.

Taken together, these titles form a comprehensive portrait of Satan's ongoing activity within the present age. They expose judicial accusation, deceptive distortion, destructive intent, illegitimate authority, and eschatological rebellion. Within the Satan–flesh–world framework, Satan emerges as the personal instigator of evil, the flesh as the internal responder to temptation, and the world as the external system that sustains rebellion.

Unless otherwise noted, Greek lexical definitions and semantic ranges in this work are drawn from *A Greek–English Lexicon of the New Testament and Other Early Christian Literature (BDAG)*, by Walter Bauer, Frederick W. Danker, William F. Arndt, and F. Wilbur Gingrich, 3rd ed. (Chicago: University of Chicago Press, 2000).

Judicial Titles: Adversary and Accuser

The name *Satan* comes from the Hebrew *śāṭān*, meaning "adversary" or "prosecutor," and carries a distinctly legal connotation.[29] In Job 1–2 and Zechariah 3:1–2, Satan appears in a courtroom setting, accusing God's servants and seeking to indict their motives and faithfulness. Revelation 12:10 explicitly identifies him as "the accuser of our brothers," situating accusation at the core of his strategy.

In the Greek New Testament, the Hebrew concept of *śāṭān* is preserved primarily through the transliteration Σατανᾶς (*Satanas*), which functions as a proper name rather than a translated term, signaling continuity with the Old Testament figure and retaining its legal-adversarial role.

Within the Satan–flesh–world framework, Satan's judicial role reveals how condemnation functions as a primary weapon. He prosecutes the believer before the conscience; the flesh internalizes guilt apart from grace; and the world reinforces shame through performance-based systems of worth. The goal is paralysis, undermining assurance, provoking despair, and weakening obedience.

In direct contrast, Jesus Christ is revealed as Advocate and Intercessor (1 John 2:1). Where Satan prosecutes, Christ defends; where Satan condemns, Christ justifies. The gospel, therefore, nullifies satanic accusation by grounding righteousness not in human performance, but in Christ's atoning work.

---

[29] Walter Bauer, Frederick W. Danker, William F. Arndt, and F. Wilbur Gingrich, *A Greek-English Lexicon of the New Testament and Other Early Christian Literature*, 3rd ed. (Chicago: University of Chicago Press, 2000), 226–227

Deceptive Titles: Devil, Serpent, and Liar

The Greek term *diabolos*, translated "devil," means "slanderer" or *"one who throws accusations,"* emphasizing deception through distortion rather than overt force. Jesus identifies Satan as "a liar and the father of lies" (John 8:44), locating deception at the center of his identity.

The title "serpent" establishes continuity between Satan's deception in Eden (Genesis 3) and his ongoing work throughout redemptive history (Revelation 12:9). His lies are rarely blatant falsehoods; they are partial truths strategically framed to appear reasonable, attractive, and even religious.

Here, the framework is especially clear: Satan initiates deception, the flesh finds the lie desirable, and the world normalizes it as wisdom. Truth is, therefore, the primary countermeasure against satanic deception. Scripture, rightly understood and obeyed, exposes lies and restores clarity to the believer's thinking (Ephesians 6:14).

Destructive Titles: Murderer and Destroyer

Jesus further identifies Satan as "a murderer from the beginning" (John 8:44), indicating that death, spiritual, relational, and ultimately physical, is the fruit of his work. Titles such as *Abaddon* or *Apollyon* ("Destroyer," Revelation 9:11) reinforce Satan's intent to corrupt, ruin, and annihilate what God has created.

Satan's destructive activity unfolds progressively. Deception leads to bondage, bondage to devastation, and devastation to death. The flesh cooperates by tolerating compromise, while the world supplies structures that conceal consequences. Scripture warns believers to resist sin at its earliest stages rather than dismissing "small" compromises that eventually yield destructive outcomes.

Cosmic Titles: Usurping Ruler and Power Broker

Scripture also assigns Satan titles describing his influence within the present world order:

- "the god of this age" (2 Corinthians 4:4)

- "the ruler of this world" (John 12:31)

- "the prince of the power of the air" (Ephesians 2:2)

These titles acknowledge real influence while carefully denying legitimate sovereignty.

Satan's authority is usurped, permitted, and temporary. He rules through deception and spiritual blindness rather than rightful dominion. Within the framework, Satan governs unseen powers; the world manifests that governance through ideologies and institutions, and the flesh adapts comfortably to those systems. Yet Scripture affirms his judgment has already been pronounced and awaits final execution: "the prince of this world now stands condemned" (John 16:11).

Eschatological Titles: Dragon, Beast, and Final Rebel

In apocalyptic literature, Satan is portrayed as the dragon, the ancient serpent, and the animating power behind beastly systems that oppose God's kingdom (Revelation 12–13). These images depict Satan as the driving force behind final rebellion, persecution, and global deception.

Significantly, Revelation emphasizes not Satan's triumph but his desperation. His rage intensifies precisely because "he knows that his time is short" (Revelation 12:12). These eschatological titles underscore the certainty of Satan's destruction rather than the permanence of his power.

Biblical nomenclature reveals Satan not as an abstract symbol, but as a personal, intelligent enemy whose activity intersects with the flesh and the world. Satan deceives, accuses, and destroys; the flesh responds and cooperates; the world amplifies and sustains rebellion. Yet every title that exposes Satan's strategy simultaneously magnifies Christ's victory. The same Scriptures that name the enemy also proclaim his defeat, assuring believers that spiritual warfare is not a struggle for victory, but a call to stand firm in a victory already secured.

Additional Names and Titles Within the Satan–Flesh–World Framework

Scripture's remaining titles for Satan further refine how his activity operates across personal, systemic, and cosmic dimensions. These names fill out the portrait already established, ensuring that no aspect of satanic strategy is left undefined.

Titles Emphasizing Predatory Threat and Ongoing Opposition

Several titles function as pastoral warnings, alerting believers to vigilance rather than speculation.

- Roaring lion (1 Peter 5:8)

- Adversary (1 Peter 5:8)

These images stress immediacy and danger. Satan is not passive; he actively seeks opportunities to devour. Within the framework, Satan hunts, the flesh grows careless, and the world distracts through comfort, noise, and false security. The command to "be sober-minded" and "watchful" assumes an intelligent predator who exploits spiritual negligence.

Titles Emphasizing Spiritual Hierarchy and Delegated Agents

Some titles expand the scope of satanic activity beyond the individual to the organized realm of spiritual powers.

- Rulers of the darkness (Ephesians 6:12)

- Ruler of the demons (Luke 11:15)

These designations clarify Satan operates through a structured kingdom of subordinates. This prevents two errors: reducing evil to human weakness alone (flesh) or attributing all suffering directly to Satan without mediation. Instead, Scripture presents layered opposition, Satan as chief rebel, subordinate powers as enforcers, the world as infrastructure, and the flesh as the internal point of access.

Titles Associated with False Worship and Corrupted Allegiance
Several names reveal Satan's aim not merely to oppose God, but to replace rightful worship.

- Beelzebub (Matthew 12:24)

- Belial (2 Corinthians 6:15)

These titles connect Satan with idolatry, moral corruption, and counterfeit authority. In the framework, Satan redirects allegiance, the flesh craves autonomy, and the world supplies alternative objects of devotion, power, pleasure, ideology, or self. Scripture, therefore, frames spiritual warfare as a conflict of worship, not merely behavior.

Titles Linked to Historical Pride and Typological Kingship
Certain Old Testament designations function typologically, drawing on historical rulers to describe satanic arrogance and rebellion.

- King of Babylon (Isaiah 14:4)

- King of Tyre (Ezekiel 28:12–17)

These titles should not be reduced to mere names we refer to, nor detached entirely from history. Rather, they reveal how satanic pride animates earthly rulers and systems. Satan's fall through self-exaltation becomes a pattern the flesh imitates, and the world celebrates. This explains why political, economic, and cultural powers often mirror the same pride, violence, and self-deification.

Titles Emphasizing Chaos, Threat, and Cosmic Disorder

- Leviathan (Isaiah 27:1)

Leviathan imagery portrays Satan as a force of chaos opposing divine order. Within redemptive history, God alone subdues Leviathan, reinforcing that Satan's defeat is not achieved through human strength but divine sovereignty. The flesh cannot conquer chaos, and the world cannot restrain it; only God can.

Titles Emphasizing False Light and Fallen Glory

- Lucifer ("Star of the morning" – Isaiah 14:12–14)
- Star fallen from heaven (Revelation 9:1)

These titles expose Satan's original temptation: exaltation apart from God. He presents himself as light while operating in darkness. The flesh resonates with this promise of self-glory, and the world rewards it through fame, dominance, and recognition. Scripture exposes this counterfeit light to prevent believers from confusing charisma with righteousness.

Titles Emphasizing End-Time Deception and Systemic Evil

- Beast (Revelation 14:9–10)
- Antichrist (1 John 4:3)
- Little horn (Daniel 8:9–11)

These titles demonstrate how satanic influence culminates in systems and figures that oppose Christ collectively rather than merely individually. Satan animates final rebellion, the world organizes it politically and culturally, and the flesh is tempted toward compromise for survival or advantage.

Taken together, the full range of biblical names and titles confirms Satan's work is comprehensive, coordinated, and persistent, yet also limited, exposed, and doomed. Satan operates as a personal deceiver and accuser, the flesh as an internal collaborator, and the world as an external amplifier. Scripture names the enemy exhaustively so that believers may neither underestimate him nor fear him excessively.

Every title that reveals Satan's strategy simultaneously points beyond him, to Christ, who has already disarmed the powers, silenced the accuser, exposed the lie, and secured final victory. Spiritual warfare is not an obsession with Satan's names, but confidence in Christ's name, which stands above every other name.

See Table A.4 in the appendix.

CHAPTER 7
THE ARMOR OF GOD AND PULLING DOWN STRONGHOLDS

The Nature of Christian Warfare: Standing and Demolishing (Ephesians 6; 2 Corinthians 10)

The New Testament presents Christian warfare through two postures. The first is standing firm against spiritual assault. And the second is actively taking down strongholds raised against the knowledge of *God*. These postures reinforce each other. Believers stand in and apply Christ's victory to thoughts, conduct, and loyalties the enemy still contests.

Paul emphasizes we do not conduct Christian warfare "according to the flesh" but with divinely empowered weapons that have spiritual effect (2 Corinthians 10:3–4). The battlefield is mostly in our minds, which involves beliefs, values, and loyalties rather than physical confrontation.

The Commander's Call: Be Strong in the Lord (Ephesians 6:10–13)

Paul's appeal begins with a command that defines the source of strength: "Be strong in the Lord and in his mighty power" (Ephesians 6:10). We cannot create strength; we receive it through union with Christ. The call to "put on the whole armor of God" shows that partial obedience leaves one spiritually vulnerable.

The Greek term (*methodiai*) describes the enemy's attacks as "schemes." This implies a careful strategy rather than random chaos. Discernment, therefore, is essential to seeing patterns of temptation, deception, and accusation.

The Belt of Truth

Truth acts as the foundation of the entire armor. Without truth, righteousness collapses, faith weakens, and assurance falters. Truth includes doctrinal accuracy, moral integrity, and relational honesty.

Satan's main weapon is deceit; therefore, truth counters his influence. Strongholds often begin with lies we tolerate rather than confront. The believer resists by identifying falsehood and submitting their thoughts and behaviors to the truth God reveals.

The Breastplate of Righteousness

The breastplate protects vital organs, symbolizing moral and spiritual integrity. Righteousness includes both *justification* (right standing before God) and *sanctification* (right living before others).

Satan accuses believers about their justification and tempts them toward sin against sanctification. Persistent, unrepentant sin creates openings for accusation and spiritual weakness. The breastplate guards the heart by grounding our identity in Christ's righteousness while calling believers to holy conduct.

Our daily life before Christ until we enter heaven should always be holy by avoiding sins. When we sin, we give the devil access. As Ephesians 4:27 tells us, "And do not give the devil a foothold." God has not called us to uncleanness, but to holiness (See 1 Thessalonians 4:7).

The Shoes of the Gospel of Peace and the Footwear of Readiness (Ephesians 6:15)

In Ephesians 6:15, the apostle Paul exhorts believers to have their feet "fitted with the readiness that comes from the gospel of peace." This imagery unites the church's missionary calling with its posture in spiritual warfare. We are to proclaim the gospel of peace, rooted in Jesus Christ's atoning sacrifice on the cross, to the whole world, especially to those who have not yet believed.

Scripture declares that whoever believes in Him will not perish but will have eternal life (John 3:16). This same gospel that reconciles sinners to God also equips believers for conflict, producing stability, readiness, and forward movement during opposition.

Paul emphasizes that peace is not the denial of warfare but the foundation on which believers stand and advance. Biblical peace (*eirēnē*) denotes reconciliation with God through Christ, resulting in a firm foundation amid hostility. Because believers are grounded in this gospel peace, accusation, fear, or suffering does not easily weaken them.

Their readiness (*hetoimasia*) reflects confidence in the reconciliation entrusted to the church. Thus, the footwear of the gospel of peace equips believers to stand firm against the enemy and faithfully proclaim Christ to a hostile world.

The Shield of Faith

"In addition to all this, take up the shield of faith, with which you can extinguish all the flaming arrows of the evil one" (Ephesians 6:16). Scripture defines faith as being confident in what we hope for and having assured conviction about what we do not yet see (Hebrews 11:1–2). This belief describes the faithful who lived before us and governed their walk before God.

In spiritual warfare, faith acts as a defensive tool that blocks every fiery assault of the evil one. These flaming missiles include deception, discouragement, accusation, fear, despair, lust, envy, and bitterness. Such attacks are destructive only when we embrace them rather than resisting.

Faith, therefore, is not mere positive thinking but a deliberate trust in God's promises and character. The Roman shield imagery underscores the communal nature of faith. This reminds believers that they can strengthen their spiritual defenses within the fellowship of the body of Christ.

The Helmet of Salvation

The helmet protects the mind, symbolizing assurance and hope. Satan targets identity and certainty to weaken our perseverance. Salvation includes present assurance and future hope, anchoring the believer amid trials.

When assurance erodes, obedience weakens. The helmet guards the believer's confidence that their salvation is secure in Christ rather than a wavering performance.

The Sword of the Spirit: The Word of God

The Word of God functions as both defensive and offensive weaponry. Jesus's temptation narrative shows. He correctly applied Scripture in obedience rather than merely quoting verses (Matthew 4:1–11).

The sword is effective when we rightly understand, internalize, and obey Scripture. Misuse of Scripture can become a tool of deception, as Satan also quotes it selectively.

Prayer at All Times

Prayer is a relational conversation between believers and God, the Creator of the universe, through which dependence, trust, and submission are continually expressed. In Ephesians 6:18, prayer functions not as an additional piece of armor but as the sustaining means by which every element of the armor is animated and rightly employed. While God remains sovereign and unrestricted in His will, Scripture consistently presents prayer as the divinely appointed means through which believers participate in His purposes.

Prayer and the Armor of God (Ephesians 6:18)

Jesus teaches believers "ought always to pray and not lose heart," grounding perseverance and spiritual endurance in continual dependence upon God rather than self-effort (Luke 18:1). Likewise, James underscores the relational dimension of prayer by observing that spiritual lack often results not from divine unwillingness but from prayerlessness (James 4:2). Jesus further affirms this posture of confident petition, calling believers to ask, seek, and knock with the assurance the Father delights in responding to His children (Matthew 7:7–11).

Prayer is neither a mechanism by which believers control God nor a passive religious ritual. Rather, it is the ordained means through which believers remain vigilant, humble, and continually reliant upon divine strength during spiritual conflict. This posture of continual dependence is captured in Paul's exhortation to "pray without ceasing," underscoring that prayer permeates the believer's life and engagement in spiritual warfare (1 Thessalonians 5:17).

CHAPTER 8
PULLING DOWN STRONGHOLDS AND SPIRITUAL WARFARE

"For though we walk in the flesh, we are not waging war according to the flesh. For the weapons of our warfare are not of the flesh but have divine power to destroy strongholds. We destroy arguments and every lofty opinion raised against the knowledge of God, and take every thought captive to obey Christ." (2 Corinthians 10:3–5)

The Teaching of Spiritual Warfare in 2 Corinthians 10:3–5
Paul depicts the Christian struggle as conducted in the sphere of human existence, yet empowered by divine resources capable of demolishing spiritual strongholds. The apostle Paul teaches that although Christians live "in the world," they do not wage war according to worldly methods. The weapons believers use are divinely empowered, capable of demolishing strongholds, overturning arguments, and taking every thought captive to obey Christ.

A. The Nature of Christian Warfare: Spiritual, Not Carnal
Paul begins by establishing a critical distinction: "For though we live in the world, we do not wage war as the world does" (2 Corinthians 10:3).

This statement affirms two truths simultaneously:

- **Believers exist within a fallen world system**, subject to cultural, social, and psychological pressures.

- **The Christian battle is not fought with human means** such as political power, coercion, violence, manipulation, or rhetorical dominance.

Christian warfare is therefore non-carnal. It is not directed against flesh and blood, nor is it advanced through human strength or strategy. This aligns with the broader New Testament teaching that the believer's struggle is against spiritual forces rather than human opponents (See Ephesians 6:12).

B. The Weapons of Our Warfare: Divinely Empowered

Paul continues: "The weapons we fight with are not the weapons of the world. On the contrary, they have divine power…" (2 Corinthians 10:4). This affirms that:

- Spiritual warfare requires <u>spiritual weapons</u>

- These weapons derive their effectiveness not from human ingenuity but from God's power

Such weapons include the Word of God, prayer, truth, obedience, faith, and the authority of Christ. These are not symbolic or metaphorical in a weak sense; they are effectual means by which God brings about spiritual victory.

C. The Meaning of "Strongholds"

Paul declares that these weapons are capable of *"demolishing strongholds."* In the Bible, strongholds are not physical structures but entrenched systems of rebellion against God, including:

- False belief systems

- Ideologies opposed to divine truth

- Cultural worldviews hostile to Christ

- Internal patterns of sin, deception, fear, or pride

Strongholds represent areas where Satan's lies have become normalized, whether in individual minds, communities, or societies.

D. The Battlefield of the Mind

Paul specifies the primary arena of warfare: "We demolish arguments and every pretension that sets itself up against the knowledge of God" (2 Corinthians 10:5). This reveals that spiritual warfare is fundamentally intellectual and moral, not merely emotional or mystical. The enemy's primary tactics are deception, false reasoning, distorted truth, and autonomous human wisdom that resist divine revelation.

Thus, Christian warfare involves:

- Confronting false doctrines

- Exposing lies

- Correcting distorted thinking

- Proclaiming truth grounded in God's revelation

E. Taking Every Thought Captive to Christ

The culmination of spiritual warfare is stated plainly: "And we take captive every thought to make it obedient to Christ" (2 Corinthians 10:5). This is one of the most theologically rich statements in Paul's teachings and discipleship. It teaches that:

- Thoughts are not morally neutral

- The mind is accountable to Christ's lordship

- True spiritual victory results in transformed thinking

To take thoughts captive means submitting:

- Reason to revelation

- Desire to obedience

- Imagination to holiness

- Intellect to Christ's authority

This reflects the New Testament vision of discipleship as total allegiance, encompassing not only actions but beliefs, attitudes, and inner reasoning.

F. Christological Focus of the Passage

The goal of spiritual warfare is not personal empowerment or psychological freedom alone, but obedience to Christ.

- Victory is defined as:

- Christ reigning in the believer's mind

- Truth overcoming deception

- God's knowledge replacing human pride

- The renewal of the inner person

Drawing on the theology of discipleship articulated by Dietrich Bonhoeffer in *The Cost of Discipleship*, this passage frames spiritual conflict as faithful obedience under the lordship of Christ rather than as sensational confrontation with demonic forces alone.[30]

G. Implications for the Church Today

Second Corinthians 10:3–5 teaches the church that:

- Spiritual warfare is primarily about truth versus deception

- The mind is a critical battleground

- Cultural ideologies must be evaluated under Christ's authority

---

[30] Dietrich Bonhoeffer, *The Cost of Discipleship*, trans. R. H. Fuller (New York: Macmillan, 1959), 45–53.

- Believers must actively resist false thinking with biblical truth

- Victory flows from submission, not spectacle

Second Corinthians 10:3–5 presents spiritual warfare as a battle for humanity's mind and allegiance. Christians fight not with worldly weapons, but with divinely empowered means that dismantle deception, expose falsehood, and bring every thought into obedience to Jesus Christ. This warfare is ongoing, disciplined, and deeply Christ-centered, rooted in truth, sustained by grace, and directed toward God's ultimate glory.

CHAPTER 9
THE UNIFIED BIBLICAL FRAMEWORK OF SPIRITUAL WARFARE

Now, if we compare these three passages of 2 Corinthians 10:3–5, Ephesians 6:10–18, and Matthew 4:1–11 together, we will see a coherent biblical doctrine of Christian spiritual warfare.

A comprehensive doctrine of Christian spiritual warfare emerges when 2 Corinthians 10:3–5, Ephesians 6:10–18, and Matthew 4:1–11 are read together. These passages do not contradict or compete with one another. Rather, they address spiritual warfare from complementary perspectives: the battlefield, the enemy, the weapons, and the model of victory in Christ.

The Nature of the Battle: Mind, Powers, and Obedience

In 2 Corinthians 10:3–5, the apostle Paul defines the conflict primarily in terms of *thought and belief*. Although believers live within the fallen world, they do not fight according to worldly patterns. The struggle involves the demolition of *strongholds*, entrenched arguments, ideologies, and pretensions that oppose the knowledge of God. The battlefield is the human mind, where deception seeks to resist the authority of Christ. Victory, therefore, is expressed as every thought we take captive into obedience to Christ.

Ephesians 6:10–18 broadens this perspective by identifying the *spiritual agents* operating behind such deception. The believer's struggle is not against human beings, but against rulers, authorities, and spiritual forces of evil in the heavenly or atmospheric realm. Here, spiritual warfare is portrayed as cosmic and organized, involving personal spiritual adversaries rather than abstract ideas alone. Paul emphasizes believers are not called to attack impulsively but to *stand firm* through divine provision.

Matthew 4:1–11 provides the historical and Christological demonstration of this warfare. In the wilderness, Satan directly confronts Jesus, not through physical force, but through temptation aimed at disobedience, presumption, and misplaced worship. The battle is intensely personal and moral, centered on whether the Son will remain obedient to the Father's will. Jesus's resistance reveals that spiritual warfare ultimately concerns allegiance and submission to God.

Taken together, these passages show that spiritual warfare involves:

- the mind (2 Corinthians 10),

- spiritual powers (Ephesians 6),

- and obedient action under temptation (Matthew 4).

The Weapons of Warfare: Divine Power, Not Human Means
Paul is explicit in 2 Corinthians 10 that the weapons of Christian warfare are not worldly but possess divine power. These weapons are effective because they originate from God and operate according to His truth. Their purpose is not the destruction of people, but the overthrow of lies and rebellion against God's revelation.

Ephesians 6 specifies these weapons metaphorically as the armor of God: truth, righteousness, the gospel of peace, faith, salvation, the Word of God, and prayer. This armor equips believers for sustained resistance and perseverance. The emphasis is not on dramatic confrontation, but on spiritual stability and endurance in the face of continual opposition.

Matthew 4 reveals how we wield these weapons in practice. Jesus responds to every temptation with Scripture, declaring, "It is written." He neither argues philosophically nor demonstrates miraculous power. Instead, He submits fully to the authority of God's Word. In doing so, Jesus exemplifies the effective use of the Sword of the Spirit and models the obedience Paul later commands believers to embrace.

Thus:

- 2 Corinthians 10 explains why spiritual weapons are effective,

- Ephesians 6 describes what those weapons are,

- Matthew 4 demonstrates how they are used.

The Goal of Spiritual Warfare: The Lordship of Christ
In all three passages, the aim of spiritual warfare is not the exaltation of the believer, nor fascination with demonic activity, but submission to Christ's lordship.

In 2 Corinthians 10, victory is defined as every thought being brought into obedience to Christ. In Ephesians 6, the goal is to stand firm in faith, righteousness, and truth until the end. In Matthew 4, Jesus's victory confirms He is the obedient Son who refuses shortcuts to glory and chooses the path of suffering obedience that leads to the cross.

Spiritual warfare, therefore, is fundamentally discipleship under pressure. It is the daily, disciplined alignment of thought, belief, and behavior with the will of God.

Christ as the Foundation and Pattern of Victory

Matthew 4 stands as the foundation upon which Paul's teaching rests. What Christ accomplished personally in the wilderness becomes the pattern and power for the church:

- Christ resisted Satan through Scripture → believers wield the Word of God

- Christ refused deception → believers demolish false arguments

- Christ stood firm in obedience → believers stand firm against spiritual forces

- Christ rejected false worship → believers submit every thought to His authority

The church does not invent its warfare strategy; it inherits it from Christ.

When read together, 2 Corinthians 10:3–5, Ephesians 6:10–18, and Matthew 4:1–11 present a unified biblical vision of spiritual warfare. The battle is spiritual rather than physical; the weapons are divine rather than human, and the victory is defined by obedience to Christ rather than domination over the enemy.

Believers engage in this warfare not in fear or uncertainty, but from a position of confidence grounded in Christ's victory. The One who triumphed in the wilderness and at the cross now reigns as Lord, empowering His people to stand firm, resist deception, and live in faithful obedience until the final defeat of Satan is fully realized.

CHAPTER 10

A DANIEL–PAUL–EPHESIANS UNIFIED WARFARE FRAMEWORK

The Anatomy of Spiritual Conflict in Scripture

Spiritual warfare in Scripture is not speculative theology but revealed reality, unfolding consistently from the Old Testament to the apostolic writings. A unified framework emerges when Daniel 10, the Pauline Epistles, and Ephesians 6 are read together. These texts reveal one continuous battlefield, governed by God's sovereignty, contested by hostile spiritual powers, and engaged by faithful obedience.

The Cosmic Realm of Warfare (Daniel)

Daniel 10 offers Scripture's clearest window into the unseen dimension of conflict. Daniel's prayer is heard immediately (Daniel 10:12), yet the answer is delayed twenty-one days due to resistance from "the prince of the Persian kingdom" (Daniel 10:13). Drawing on the divine-council framework articulated by Old Testament scholar Michael S. Heiser in *The Unseen Realm*, spiritual beings are portrayed as exercising delegated authority over the nations, yet always under the ultimate sovereignty of the God of Israel.[31]

---

[31] Michael S. Heiser, *The Unseen Realm: Recovering the Supernatural Worldview of the Bible* (Bellingham, WA: Lexham Press, 2015), 113–120.

This establishes several foundational truths:

1 Spiritual beings exercise delegated influence over earthly realms. Prayer activates movement in the heavenly realm.

2 Angelic conflict occurs beyond human perception.

3 God's purposes advance through conflict, not despite it.

Daniel does not confront the demonic power directly. Instead, angelic intervention (Michael) resolves the resistance, demonstrating that authority over principalities belongs to God alone. Human responsibility is persistence, humility, and faith, not domination.

Daniel, therefore, supplies the cosmic context of warfare: invisible, structured, and real.

Satanic Hindrance in Apostolic Ministry (Paul)

The apostolic experience of warfare is particularly evident in the ministry of Paul, where satanic opposition manifests not only in external persecution but in strategic hindrance to the advancement of the gospel. Paul's ministry reflects the reality of the warfare Daniel glimpsed. Paul moves from revelation to experience, naming the enemy and its effects without sensationalism. "But we, brethren, being taken from you for a short time in presence, not in heart, endeavored the more abundantly to see your face with great desire. Wherefore we would have come unto you, even I Paul, once and again; but Satan hindered us" (1 Thessalonians 2:17–18).

Paul's assertion in 1 Thessalonians 2:18, "Satan hindered us," is one of the most explicit apostolic acknowledgments that Christian mission operates within an arena of real spiritual conflict. The verb Paul uses (*enkoptō*, "to cut into, block, obstruct") was commonly employed for destroying a road to halt an advancing army. Paul understood satanic opposition not as abstract temptation alone, but as strategic interference aimed at disrupting the advancement of the gospel and pastoral presence.

This theme is not isolated. Across Paul's letters, satanic activity consistently appears as an adversarial force seeking to delay, deceive, weaken, divide, or afflict, always operating within God's sovereign limits, never as an equal rival.

In 2 Corinthians 2:11, Paul warns that believers must remain vigilant "so that Satan might not outwit us," revealing Satan employs schemes (*noēmata*), calculated strategies rather than random assaults. These schemes often target relationships, forgiveness, unity, and discernment, precisely the areas essential for healthy church life and effective ministry.

Similarly, 2 Corinthians 12:7 introduces the paradox of satanic affliction under divine permission: "a messenger of Satan to torment me." Here, hindrance takes the form of personal suffering, not to destroy Paul, but to humble him and magnify divine grace. Satan intends harm; God redeems the affliction for sanctification and apostolic endurance.

Paul also recognizes satanic exploitation of human weakness. In 1 Corinthians 7:5, Satan seeks to gain advantage through disordered desires, turning neglect of spiritual discipline into an entry point for temptation. Thus, satanic hindrance may occur not only through persecution but also through moral vulnerability within the Christian life.

Paul frames all such experiences within a cosmic framework. Ephesians 6:12 clarifies that apostolic struggle is never merely circumstantial or human: "Our struggle is not against flesh and blood." What appears as travel disruption, opposition, illness, or relational strain is often the surface manifestation of deeper spiritual resistance.

Taken together, Paul's theology presents Satan as a real but restrained adversary, capable of hindering ministry temporarily, yet incapable of overturning God's redemptive purposes. Hindrance is real; defeat is not final.

Paul's theology thus expands Daniel's vision:

- Daniel reveals where warfare occurs.

- Paul explains how it is experienced in ministry, suffering, relationships, and mission.

The Believer's Posture in Warfare (Ephesians)

While Daniel reveals the unseen realm and Paul narrates apostolic engagement, Ephesians 6:10–18 instructs the church how to stand within it.

Paul clarifies the enemy: "Our struggle is not against flesh and blood" (Ephesians 6:12).

In his commentary on Colossians and Ephesians, F. F. Bruce explains that Paul's use of terms such as "rulers" (*archai*) and "authorities" (*exousiai*) denotes real spiritual powers within the created order, all of which are ultimately subjected to the supreme lordship of Christ.[32] This conceptual framework resonates with the portrayal of spiritual conflict in Daniel 10. The pastoral emphasis, however, is decisive: believers are not instructed to confront these powers directly, but to stand firm in the victory secured in Christ.

The armor of God is defensive and formative:

---

[32] F. F. Bruce, *The Epistles to the Colossians, to Philemon, and to the Ephesians*, New International Commentary on the New Testament (Grand Rapids, MI: Eerdmans, 1984), 61;.

- Truth stabilizes the mind.

- Righteousness guards moral integrity.

- Faith extinguishes satanic accusation.

- Salvation anchors identity.

- The Word resists deception.

- Prayer sustains engagement.

Ephesians does not deny warfare; it assumes it, but locates victory in union with Christ, not in human aggression.

See Table A.5 in the appendix.

Synthetic Pauline Principles
Satan hinders servants, not the sovereignty of God.

1 Hindrance often intensifies where ministry is most fruitful.

2 Discernment and perseverance are primary apostolic responses.

God transforms satanic opposition into instruments of maturity.

Theological Conclusions

1 Spiritual warfare is real, structured, and continuous throughout Scripture.

2 Prayer initiates movement in the unseen realm.

3 Satan can hinder timing, never destiny.

4 Believers do not fight for victory but from victory in Christ.

5 Perseverance, holiness, and truth are the church's primary weapons.

Daniel reveals the battlefield, Paul reveals the cost, and Ephesians reveals the stance. Together, they form a unified biblical theology in which spiritual warfare is neither exaggerated nor ignored. Rather, it is rightly understood as the context in which faithful obedience unfolds under God's sovereign rule.

Having examined the external enemy (Satan) and the means of resistance, we now turn inward to *the flesh*, the internal enemy that remains active even in regenerated believers.

CHAPTER 11
OUR SECOND ENEMY: THE FLESH— THE INTERNALIZATION OF CONFLICT

The expulsion from Eden introduces the theme of exile, which becomes a controlling motif throughout redemptive history. Humanity's removal from God's presence results not only in geographical displacement but also in moral and spiritual corruption.

The apostle Paul describes this fallen condition as "The Flesh," the internal power of sin that resists God's law and frustrates obedience (Romans 7:18–25; Galatians 5:17). Drawing on T. Desmond Alexander's theology of exile, the flesh may be understood as an internal enemy that perpetuates humanity's alienation from God. Humanity's expulsion east of Eden signifies the loss of its original priestly vocation and separation from the divine presence, marking the beginning of a sustained condition of exile that the biblical narrative progressively addresses.[33] This rupture produces an inward disorder that Scripture later describes as "The Flesh," explaining why even regenerate believers experience ongoing conflict between desire and obedience. This biblical-theological insight coheres directly with Paul's teaching that we do not achieve victory over the flesh through self-effort or

---

[33] T. Desmond Alexander, *From Eden to the New Jerusalem: An Introduction to Biblical Theology* (Grand Rapids, MI: Kregel, 2008), 98–105.

legalism, but through life in the Spirit made possible by union with Christ (Romans 8:1–11).

Scripture presents the flesh (our Adamic nature) as a persistent internal adversary that remains active even after conversion. While Satan functions as an external personal enemy, the flesh represents the inherited fallen nature that resists the Spirit of God from within. Paul exhorts believers to "Walk by the Spirit, and you will not gratify the desires of the flesh" (Galatians 5:16).

Also, the Bible states in Romans 8:9–13 (emphasis mine):

You, however, are not in the realm of the flesh but are in the realm of the Spirit, if indeed the Spirit of God lives in you. And if anyone does not have the Spirit of Christ, they do not belong to Christ.

But if Christ is in you, then even though your body is subject to death because of sin, the Spirit gives life because of righteousness. And if the Spirit of Him who raised Jesus from the dead is living in you, He who raised Christ from the dead will also give life to your mortal bodies because of His Spirit who lives in you.

Therefore, brothers and sisters, we have an obligation, but it is not to the flesh, to live according to it. For if you live according to the flesh, you will die; but if by the Spirit you put to death the misdeeds of the body, you will live.

The flesh is not morally neutral weakness but an active principle of opposition to God. It resists submission, distorts desire, and seeks autonomy apart from divine authority. Spiritual warfare, therefore, involves not only resisting satanic attacks but also mortifying fleshly impulses that contradict the will of God.

The Flesh of Man: Definition and Origin

The New Testament term translated "flesh" derives from the Greek *sarx*, which refers not merely to the physical body but to the fallen human nature inherited from Adam. Scripture consistently portrays *sarx* as hostile to God and incapable of submitting to His law (Romans 8:6–8). As Douglas J. Moo explains in his commentary on Romans, particularly in his exposition of Romans 7:14–25 and 8:1–13, the term sarx ("flesh") does not denote the physical body as such but refers to the whole person in Adam, oriented in opposition to God and existing under the power of sin.[34]

"Those who live according to the flesh have their minds set on what the flesh desires; but those who live in accordance with the Spirit have their minds set on what the Spirit desires. The mind governed by the flesh is death, but the mind governed by the Spirit is life and peace. The mind governed by the flesh is hostile to God; it does not submit to God's law, nor can it do so. Those who are in the realm of the flesh cannot please God" (Romans 8:5–8).

The flesh is also described as:

The Sinful Nature

This phrase emphasizes the moral corruption inherited through the fall.

- Romans 7:18 "For I know that good itself does not dwell in me, that is, in my sinful nature. For I have the desire to do what is good, but I cannot carry it out."

- Galatians 5:17 "For the flesh desires what is contrary to the Spirit, and the Spirit what is contrary to the flesh."

---

[34] Douglas J. Moo, *The Epistle to the Romans*, New International Commentary on the New Testament (Grand Rapids: Eerdmans, 1996).

The Old Man

This term refers to the former identity and way of life before union with Christ.

- Ephesians 4:22 "You were taught, regarding your former way of life, to put off your old self, which is being corrupted by its deceitful desires."

The Old Adamic Nature (Our Sinful Inheritance)

- Romans 5:12: "Therefore, just as sin entered the world through one man, and death through sin, and in this way death came to all people, because all sinned."

- 1 Corinthians 15:22: "For as in Adam all die, so in Christ all will be made alive."

- Ephesians 2:1–3: "As for you, you were dead in your transgressions and sins, in which you used to live when you followed the ways of this world and of the ruler of the kingdom of the air, the spirit who is now at work in those who are disobedient. All of us also lived among them at one time, gratifying the cravings of our flesh and following its desires and thoughts. Like the rest, we were by nature deserving of wrath."

- Romans 8:7: "The mind controlled by the flesh is hostile to God… it does not submit to God's law, nor can it do so."

The Body of Death (The Struggle with Sin)

- Romans 7:24–25: "What a wretched man I am! Who will rescue me from this body that is subject to death? Thanks be to God, through Jesus Christ our Lord!"

- Romans 6:6: "For we know that our old self was crucified with him so that the body ruled by sin might be done away with, that we should no longer be slaves to sin" (Believers are crucified with Christ, ending slavery to sin).

- Colossians 3:5: "Put to death, therefore, your earthly nature: sexual immorality, impurity, lust, evil desires and greed, which is idolatry" (Command to actively deal with sinful desires).

- Galatians 5:24: "Those who belong to Christ Jesus have crucified the flesh with its passions and desires" (Believers have crucified the flesh through Christ).

These terms emphasize that the flesh is not a collection of habits, but a governing principle rooted in humanity's fallen condition.

CHAPTER 12
MAN BEFORE AND AFTER THE FALL

The Reordering of Human Nature and the Dominion of the Flesh
This chapter examines the reordering of human nature brought
about by the fall, with particular focus on the emergence of the
flesh as a governing principle that cannot be reformed. Scripture
presents man as created in an ordered unity of spirit, soul, and
body, designed for communion with God and directed toward His
glory. Prior to the fall, the human spirit functioned in rightful
orientation under God, governing the soul and body and ordering
desire and action in accordance with divine truth.

The fall introduced a decisive inversion of this order. Genesis
3:6 traces the progression of temptation through disordered desire:
"good for food" (the appetites of the body), "pleasing to the eye"
(the affections of the soul), and "desirable for gaining wisdom"
(the assertion of autonomous judgment). In this moment, the
spirit's submission to God was abandoned, the soul aligned with
distorted desire, and the body became the instrument of
disobedience.

As a result, human existence came under the dominion of the
flesh rather than the Spirit. This condition is not superficial but
structural, affecting the orientation of the entire person. Genesis
6:3 reflects this shift, indicating that humanity now exists in a state

defined by mortality and corruption, where the flesh governs in opposition to the life of the Spirit.

Divine Grief, Human Corruption, and the Redemptive Trajectory Toward Christ (Genesis 6:1–3, 5–7; Canonical Horizon: Romans 8)

Genesis 6 marks a decisive escalation in the reordering of human nature introduced by the fall. What began in Genesis 3 as disordered desire now appears as pervasive corruption, revealing the full dominion of the flesh over human existence. Humanity's numerical expansion is matched by moral collapse, indicating that the spread of sin is not incidental but systemic. The text's assessment is comprehensive: "every inclination of the thoughts of the human heart was only evil continually" (Genesis 6:5). Sin is therefore not presented as occasional failure but as a settled disposition of the human will. This passage establishes a biblical anthropology[35] in which corruption proceeds from the inner life, demonstrating that the disorder introduced by the fall has become the governing condition of humanity.

The divine response is described in strikingly personal terms: "the LORD regretted that he had made humankind on the earth, and it grieved him to his heart" (Genesis 6:6). The Hebrew verb nā◉am (נחם) carries a broad semantic range, including grief, sorrow, relenting, and deep emotional pain. This language does not imply divine ignorance or a revision of prior intent. Rather, it expresses God's holy sorrow in response to real historical wickedness. The description is best understood as

---

[35] Theological anthropology is the branch of theology that examines the nature of humanity as created in the image of God, the structure of human existence (such as spirit, soul, and body), the effects of sin on that nature, and the implications of redemption through Christ.

anthropomorphic[36] and anthropopathic[37] accommodation, through which God reveals His moral posture toward sin in forms accessible to human understanding.

Anthropomorphic language attributes human form or action to God, while anthropopathic language attributes human emotions to God; both function as accommodated expressions that communicate divine reality in human terms. This grief must be interpreted in light of God's unchanging nature. Scripture affirms that God does not change in essence, character, or ultimate purpose (Numbers 23:19; Malachi 3:6). The "regret" of Genesis 6, therefore, reflects not instability in God but consistency: the unchanging God who eternally loves righteousness must oppose persistent corruption. What changes is not God's nature, but humanity's covenantal standing before Him. As rebellion intensifies, divine judgment emerges as the necessary expression of divine holiness in response to a world now governed by disordered desire.

The flood judgment that follows is thus neither impulsive nor arbitrary. It is a measured act of divine justice directed against a world saturated with violence, corruption, and moral disorder. Significantly, the judgment extends beyond humanity to the created order itself (Genesis 6:7), indicating that human sin carries cosmic consequences. Creation suffers because humanity, its appointed steward, has become fundamentally disordered, and

---

[36] Anthropomorphic, (*From Greek: anthrōpos = human and morphē = form*), language refers to the attribution of human physical characteristics or actions to God in order to communicate divine activity in forms understandable to human beings

[37] Anthropopathic, (*From Greek: anthrōpos = human and pathos = emotion / feeling*), language refers to the attribution of human emotions or affections to God in order to express His moral response to human actions in ways intelligible to human understanding.

the effects of this disorder extend outward into the fabric of the created world.

This creational dimension of sin and judgment is taken up and developed by the apostle Paul in Romans 8. Paul teaches that "creation was subjected to futility" and now exists in "bondage to corruption," groaning as it awaits redemption (Romans 8:19–23). Genesis 6 narrates the historical manifestation of this corruption; Romans 8 provides its theological interpretation. As Douglas J. Moo explains in his commentary on Romans, human sin fractures not only the relationship between God and humanity but the integrity of creation itself, confirming that the effects of sin extend beyond the individual to encompass the entire created order (cf. Romans 8:19–23).[38]

Yet Genesis 6 is not solely a narrative of judgment; it is also a narrative of preservation. "But Noah found favor in the eyes of the LORD" (Genesis 6:8). Divine judgment is never the final word. Even as God acts decisively against corruption, He preserves a righteous remnant through whom His redemptive purposes continue. This pattern, judgment coupled with preservation, establishes a typological trajectory that reaches its fulfillment in Jesus Christ.

Romans 8 announces the decisive resolution to the condition Genesis 6 exposes: "There is therefore now no condemnation for those who are in Christ Jesus" (Romans 8:1).God has done what the law, weakened by the flesh, could not accomplish: He sent His Son "in the likeness of sinful flesh" and "condemned sin in the flesh" (Romans 8:3). As Douglas J. Moo explains, this text reveals that God executed judgment on sin through the person of Christ

---

[38] Douglas J. Moo, *The Epistle to the Romans*, New International Commentary on the New Testament (Grand Rapids, MI: Eerdmans, 1996), 513–517.

rather than upon the sinner.[39] Where Genesis 6 depicts sin judged through the destruction of the world, Romans 8 reveals sin condemned through the crucifixion of Christ. In this way, judgment is no longer borne by creation but is absorbed by the Son on behalf of His people.

This Christological fulfillment also clarifies the role of the Spirit. In Genesis 6:3, God declares that His Spirit will not contend with humanity indefinitely, indicating a limit to divine forbearance in the face of entrenched rebellion. Romans 8 presents the redemptive counterpoint: the Spirit now indwells believers, liberating them from the dominion of the flesh and empowering a new mode of life oriented toward God (Romans 8:2–13). As Gordon D. Fee explains, life in the Spirit marks the decisive transition from bondage to freedom in Christ.[40] What was withdrawn in judgment is now poured out in redemption.

Finally, the flood narrative functions typologically. Peter explicitly connects Noah's deliverance through water with salvation accomplished through Christ's resurrection (1 Peter 3:20–21).[41] As Karen H. Jobes explains, Noah's passage through the waters of judgment prefigures the believer's salvation through union with Christ. As Noah emerges into a renewed world, so believers pass from condemnation into new life, awaiting the final liberation of creation promised in Romans 8:21.[42] Genesis 6

---

[39] Douglas J. Moo, *The Epistle to the Romans*, NICNT (Grand Rapids, MI: Eerdmans, 1996), 480–485.

[40] Gordon D. Fee, *God's Empowering Presence: The Holy Spirit in the Letters of Paul* (Peabody, MA: Hendrickson, 1994), 505–510.

[41] Karen H. Jobes, *1 Peter*, Baker Exegetical Commentary on the New Testament (Grand Rapids, MI: Baker Academic, 2005), 240–245.

[42] Douglas J. Moo, *The Epistle to the Romans*, NICNT (Grand Rapids, MI: Eerdmans, 1996), 515–518.

therefore, anticipates the gospel: God's grief over sin leads not only to judgment but ultimately to a redemptive act that secures both human salvation and cosmic renewal.

This passage thus prepares the theological ground for the book's later conclusion: the enemies of humanity, sin, the flesh, and the corrupted world order, are real and devastating, but they are not ultimate. In Christ, judgment has been executed, the Spirit has been given, and creation itself is destined for freedom and glory (Romans 8:30).

See Table A.6 in the appendix.

Unified Operation, Distinct Functions

Genesis 6 shows that Satan, the flesh, and the world do not operate independently:

- Satan exploits disorder and boundary transgression.

- The flesh provides the internal consent and inclination toward evil.

- The world becomes the external system saturated with corruption.

Together, they form a self-reinforcing triad of rebellion.

The Adamic Nature—the Flesh, Satan, and the Ground of Assurance

Everything occurring in the world today, nations rising against nations, people turning against one another, and societies marked by greed, hatred, selfish ambition, pride, deception, theft, and sexual immorality, reflects humanity's fallen condition. These evils are the outworking of the Adamic nature, expressed through the flesh, and strategically exploited by Satan the devil, who operates subtly and often unseen to deceive and corrupt God's creation. At the root of this condition stands the Adamic nature, the inherited state of humanity resulting from Adam's disobedience, through which sin and death entered the human experience (Romans 5:12). This nature defines humanity's fallen status before God: a condition of spiritual alienation and moral inability apart from grace. The Adamic nature explains *why* humanity is enslaved to sin, but it does not negate God's redemptive initiative nor determine the final destiny of those who are in Christ.

Flowing from this fallen condition is the flesh, which represents the expression of the Adamic nature in human desires, affections, and behaviors. The flesh is the internal battleground where sinful impulses oppose God's will and resist the Holy Spirit's sanctifying work (Romans 7:14–25; Galatians 5:16–21). Scripture presents the struggle with the flesh not as evidence of spiritual defeat but as a mark of spiritual life. The conflict presupposes the presence of the Spirit and anticipates transformation through ongoing sanctification (see Chapter 6). Thus, the believer's warfare with the flesh must be understood within the larger framework of assurance, not condemnation.

Satan, the devil, operates as a distinct and external adversary within this conflict. He is neither the source of the Adamic nature nor the origin of sinful desire, but the chief manipulator of both. Through deception, accusation, and temptation, Satan seeks to exploit the flesh and reinforce the values of the fallen world system to undermine confidence in God's promises (See Chapter 3). A central element of Satan's strategy is not simply to entice believers into sin, but to erode their assurance by magnifying failure and obscuring the sufficiency of Christ's finished work.

For this reason, careful theological distinction is essential. The Adamic nature explains humanity's need for salvation, the flesh explains the believer's ongoing struggle, and Satan explains the external pressure that seeks to destabilize faith. Yet none of these realities possesses ultimate authority over those in Christ. Scripture consistently locates the believer's confidence not in the absence of conflict, but in the certainty of divine victory. The presence of warfare does not negate assurance; rather, it presupposes the believer belongs to Christ and stands in opposition to hostile powers.

This doctrinal clarity prepares the reader for the book's concluding emphasis on assurance and perseverance in Christ. The Adamic nature has been decisively judged through union with Christ, the power of the flesh has been rendered non-determinative through the indwelling Spirit, and Satan's authority has been legally disarmed through the cross and resurrection (Romans 5:18–19; Galatians 5:24–25; Colossians 2:13–15). Consequently, perseverance is not grounded in human strength or moral perfection, but in God's preserving grace and Christ's ongoing intercession. Spiritual warfare, rightly understood, does not threaten the believer's security; it confirms the reality of redemption and directs the believer to rest fully in the triumph of Christ.

The Unchangeable and Irreparable Nature of the Flesh
Jesus declares an unalterable principle: "That which is born of the flesh is flesh" (John 3:6). The flesh cannot be improved, repaired, educated, changed, disciplined, or sanctified through human effort. Scripture nowhere teaches the reform of the flesh; it teaches its condemnation.

Because the flesh is irreparable, God's solution is not rehabilitation but crucifixion. The cross does not polish the old nature; it executes it. Any theology that promises moral transformation apart from death to the flesh undermines the gospel.

If the flesh cannot be reformed, then victory in spiritual warfare cannot begin with discipline or resistance, but with new birth. This brings us to regeneration.

CHAPTER 13
REGENERATION: THE FOUNDATIONAL VICTORY OF SPIRITUAL WARFARE

What Is Regeneration: God's Answer to the Flesh
At conversion, God accomplishes a radical internal transformation known as regeneration. When a person believes in Christ, the Holy Spirit imparts new life, creating a new nature oriented toward God (John 3:3–8).

Regeneration as the Gateway to Victory
Regeneration, or the new birth, is the foundation of Christian spiritual warfare. Before the believer can engage the enemies of the soul, Satan, the flesh, and the world, they must first be spiritually made alive by God. Jesus declares, "Unless one is born again, he cannot see the kingdom of God" (John 3:3). This statement establishes regeneration not as optional, but as an absolute prerequisite for salvation, discernment, and spiritual authority.

Without regeneration, humanity remains spiritually blind, enslaved to sin, and subject to the dominion of darkness. Therefore, spiritual warfare does not begin with resistance; it begins with resurrection.

Regeneration as Divine Recreation
Regeneration is the Holy Spirit's sovereign work, whereby God recreates the inner person, imparting His life to the believer (John

3:6; Titus 3:5). This is not moral reform or religious adjustment; it is a supernatural transformation. The believer becomes a new creation in Christ, no longer defined by Adamic corruption but by divine life (2 Corinthians 5:17).

This inward renewal confronts this enemy, "the flesh." Where the unregenerate person is governed by sinful inclinations and hostile to God (Romans 8:7–8), the regenerated believer receives a new disposition of righteousness and holiness (Ephesians 4:24). Thus, regeneration breaks the internal stronghold that Satan exploits most effectively: the fallen nature.

Regeneration and Deliverance from Satan's Dominion

Regeneration also marks a decisive transfer of allegiance. Scripture consistently portrays salvation as deliverance from the kingdom of darkness into the kingdom of Christ (Colossians 1:13). Those who are born again become children of God, no longer children of wrath or captives of Satan (John 1:12; Romans 8:16–17).

This has direct implications for spiritual warfare. Satan's authority operates over the unregenerate world system and over those who walk according to the flesh (Ephesians 2:1–3). Regeneration severs this dominion. While Satan continues to oppose believers through temptation, accusation, and deception, his legal claim is broken. The regenerated believer now stands in Christ's victory and resists the devil not as a slave seeking freedom, but as a son defending his inheritance.

Repentance and Faith as the Human Response

Although regeneration is God's work alone, He grants it to those who respond in repentance and faith. Turning from sin and placing personal trust in Jesus Christ is the divinely appointed way a believer receives the new birth (Matthew 3:2; John 1:12). This repentance goes beyond emotional remorse to a decisive renunciation of the old life, the world's values, the rule of the flesh, and the lies of Satan.

Repentance functions as an act of warfare: a conscious break with the enemy's territory and an entry into Christ's kingdom.

Regeneration and the New Pattern of Life

The regenerated believer does not simply profess faith but manifests transformation. Scripture affirms that those born of God live righteously, love fellow believers, reject habitual sin, and refuse devotion to the world system (1 John 2:29; 3:9; 4:7; 2:15–16). This does not imply sinless perfection, but it demands spiritual direction and obedience.

The Work of Regeneration

Regeneration directly confronts the second and third enemies: The flesh is no longer master but must be crucified daily. The world is no longer loved but discerned and resisted.

A life persistently showing immorality and conformity to the world exposes the absence of regeneration, regardless of verbal profession. In warfare terms, such a life reveals continued occupation by the enemy.

Dear children, do not let anyone lead you astray. The one who does what is right is righteous, just as he is righteous. The one who does what is sinful is of the devil, because the devil has been sinning from the beginning. The reason the Son of God appeared was to destroy the devil's work. No one who is born of God will continue to sin, because God's seed remains in them; they cannot go on sinning, because they have been born of God. This is how we know who the children of God are and who the children of the devil are: Anyone who does not do what is right is not God's child, nor is anyone who does not love their brother and sister. (1 John 3:7–10)

Perseverance, the Spirit, and Ongoing Warfare
Regeneration initiates spiritual life, but continued victory requires dependence on the Holy Spirit. Scripture warns that spiritual life can be quenched through persistent disobedience and refusal to walk by the Spirit (Romans 8:13). While physical birth cannot be undone, the spiritual relationship with God remains relational and covenantal, requiring perseverance in faith and obedience.

This sobering truth reinforces a central theme of this manuscript: spiritual warfare is not theoretical but existential. Eternal life is lived, guarded, and expressed through daily submission to Christ and reliance on the Spirit.

Regeneration as the Strategic Center of Christian Warfare
In summary, regeneration is the:

- Defeat of Satan's legal authority

- Death blow to the flesh's dominion

- Separation from the world's system

- Birth of a warrior-son or daughter of God

Without regeneration, there is no true resistance. With regeneration, the believer does not fight for victory but from victory, grounded in the life of God and empowered by the Spirit of Christ.

Scripture teaches believers become "partakers of the divine nature" (2 Peter 1:4). Regeneration restores the human spirit, enabling communion with God and obedience empowered by grace.

This transformation is not an emotional sensation but a spiritual recreation. Knowing the truth about Christ without personally trusting Him from the heart does not bring about spiritual rebirth (Romans 10:9–10).

CHAPTER 14
TWO NATURES IN THE BELIEVER

Following regeneration, the believer enters a state of internal conflict marked by the coexistence of two opposing principles: the flesh and the new life of the Spirit. This tension is inherent to the present condition of redeemed humanity. The flesh, understood as the Adamic nature inherited through the fall, remains active, exerting influence through disordered desires and resistance to God. In contrast, the regenerated self-delights in God's law and is oriented toward righteousness. The conflict described in Romans 7 therefore reflects not spiritual failure, but the reality of new life contending against the residual presence of sin.

The Law of Sin and the Inability of the Flesh

Paul identifies within the believer a governing principle he calls "the law of sin" operating in the members (Romans 7:21–23). This law operates as a structural principle, exerting influence through the body and soul in an effort to reassert dominance. The result is a persistent tension between desire and action: the renewed mind affirms what is good, yet the flesh resists its execution.

This condition reveals a critical theological truth: the flesh is not reformable. It cannot be improved through discipline, corrected through moral effort, or brought into alignment with God's will through human resolve. The inability described in Romans 7 is not the failure of effort but the limitation of nature.

The flesh lacks both the capacity and the inclination to submit to God.

The Function of the Law: Revelation Without Liberation

Paul further clarifies the role of the Mosaic Law. The law is holy, righteous, and good, yet it functions as a revelatory instrument rather than a redemptive power. Through the commandment, sin is exposed, defined, and intensified. As Paul writes, "I would not have known what sin was had it not been for the law" (Romans 7:7).

The law, therefore, does not produce righteousness; it reveals the depth of unrighteousness. Sin seizes the commandment as an opportunity, producing transgression and exposing the internal corruption of the human condition. What was intended for life becomes the occasion for death, not because of any defect in the law, but because of the sinful nature that encounters it.

The extended testimony of Romans 7:4–25 provides a detailed account of this conflict:

The Crisis of the Human Condition

The culmination of this internal struggle is expressed in Paul's cry: "What a wretched man I am! Who will rescue me from this body that is subject to death?" (Romans 7:24). This statement captures the existential reality of the believer confronted with the persistent presence of indwelling sin. The problem is not external circumstance but internal corruption. The flesh remains an active principle of opposition, incapable of submission to God and resistant to transformation.

The law exposes this condition, but it cannot resolve it. Moral resolve proves insufficient, and self-effort results in frustration rather than freedom. The conflict, therefore, drives the believer away from self-reliance and toward the necessity of divine intervention.

Deliverance Through Christ and Life in the Spirit
The answer to this crisis is not found within the self but in Jesus Christ. Paul's declaration, "Thanks be to God, who delivers me through Jesus Christ our Lord!" (Romans 7:25), marks the decisive transition from struggle to solution. Deliverance is not achieved but received, founded in the atoning work of Christ and applied through union with Him.

Romans 8 provides the theological resolution to the tension described in chapter 7. "There is therefore now no condemnation for those who are in Christ Jesus" (Romans 8:1). The believer is no longer under the law of sin and death but lives under the law of the Spirit of life. What the law could not accomplish, weakened by the flesh, God has accomplished through His Son.

This transformation does not eliminate the presence of the flesh, but it decisively breaks its dominion. The believer's identity is no longer defined by the flesh but by the Spirit. To be "in the Spirit" is to belong to Christ, to be indwelt by the Spirit of God, and to participate in the life secured through His resurrection.

Conclusion: Conflict Clarified, Victory Defined
The tension described in Romans 7 does not excuse sin but clarifies the source of the struggle. The presence of conflict confirms the reality of regeneration, while the persistence of sin exposes the continuing influence of the flesh. Victory, therefore, does not come through willpower, but through participation in the life of the Spirit.

As Paul exhorts in Galatians 5:16, "walk by the Spirit, and you will not gratify the desires of the flesh." The Christian life is not the reform of the old nature, but the outworking of a new one. The flesh remains irreparable, but its authority is broken. Freedom is found not in self-mastery, but in union with Christ and dependence upon the Spirit.

The internal conflict described in Romans 7 does not remain concealed within the believer but manifests outwardly in observable patterns of conduct. The presence of the flesh is revealed not only through inward resistance to God's law but through actions that reflect its governing influence. Scripture, therefore, moves from diagnosis to exposure, identifying the concrete expressions of this inner disorder. These manifestations are explicitly cataloged in Galatians 5:19–21 as the works of the flesh.

CHAPTER 15
The Works of the Flesh

The internal conflict described in Romans 7 does not remain hidden within the believer but becomes visible through concrete patterns of conduct. The flesh, as an active and opposing principle, expresses itself in actions that reveal its governing influence. Scripture therefore moves from the internal reality of struggle to the external evidence of disorder, identifying these expressions as the works of the flesh.

"The acts of the flesh are obvious: sexual immorality, impurity, and debauchery; idolatry and witchcraft; hatred, discord, jealousy, fits of rage, selfish ambition, dissensions, factions and envy; drunkenness, orgies, and the like. I warn you, as I did before, that those who live like this will not inherit the kingdom of God" (Galatians 5:19–21).

The Works of the Flesh as Manifestation of Inner Corruption
Paul's catalog presents more than a list of individual sins; it offers a theological diagnosis of a life governed by the flesh. These works function as the fruit of a corrupted nature, revealing the outward expression of an inward condition. They are not isolated acts but recurring patterns that disclose the controlling principle of the heart.

As John Calvin observes in *Institutes of the Christian Religion* (1.11.8), "the human mind is, so to speak, a perpetual forge of idols." External behaviors, therefore, constitute the visible expression of an inward disorder rooted in the human heart, a reality that Scripture itself locates at the core of human corruption (Mark 7:21–23).[43] The works of the flesh expose the condition of a nature that has turned from God and now operates in opposition to His will.

The Flesh as the Internal Battlefield

Among the three enemies confronting the believer, Satan, the flesh, and the world; the flesh constitutes the most immediate and persistent battlefield. Unlike Satan, who opposes from without, or the world, which exerts pressure from around, the flesh operates from within, shaping desires, distorting judgment, and directing the will away from God.

The conflict described in Galatians 5:16–17 establishes that the Christian life is defined by opposition. The flesh resists the Spirit, and the Spirit opposes the flesh, producing an ongoing struggle that characterizes the believer's present experience. This tension reflects the presence of new life contending against the residual influence of the old nature.

The Flesh and Satan's Strategy

Satan's strategy against the believer operates through the internal dynamics of the flesh. Scripture teaches that temptation arises as desire is drawn out and enticed (James 1:14–15). As Douglas J. Moo explains in his commentary on James, the source of temptation resides within the disordered desires of the human heart. External enticement, therefore, finds its efficacy in an already corrupted internal disposition.[44]

---

[43] John Calvin, *Institutes of the Christian Religion*, ed. John T. McNeill, trans. Ford Lewis Battles (Louisville: Westminster John Knox Press, 1960), 1.11.8.

[44] Douglas J. Moo, *The Letter of James*, New International Commentary on the New Testament (Grand Rapids: Eerdmans, 2000), **73–75**.

The works of the flesh, therefore, constitute the operational terrain through which destructive influence advances. Practices such as sexual immorality, idolatry, hostility, jealousy, and drunkenness function as patterns that reinforce bondage and weaken resistance. These behaviors are not neutral; they align the believer with forces that oppose God's purposes. Victory over Satan is thus inseparably connected to the mortification of the flesh.

The Flesh and the World System

The flesh does not operate in isolation but is reinforced by the world system, which normalizes sin, celebrates self-indulgence, and resists divine authority. The world supplies the values, the flesh supplies the desires, and Satan supplies the deception. Together, they form a coordinated opposition to holiness.

Paul's warning is therefore direct: those who habitually practice the works of the flesh will not inherit the kingdom of God (Galatians 5:21). This warning does not suggest that salvation is earned by works, but that persistent, unrepentant patterns of fleshly living reveal an allegiance that remains aligned with the world rather than with Christ.

The Works of the Flesh as Evidence of Spiritual Defeat

The works of the flesh function as a diagnostic instrument within the framework of spiritual warfare. These behaviors are not incidental lapses but patterns that signal the governing influence of the old nature. When allowed to dominate, they dull spiritual perception, weaken resistance to temptation, and erode fellowship with God.

In this sense, these works reveal more than moral failure; they expose spiritual misalignment. The believer who yields to the flesh does not lose salvation, but forfeits experiential victory, surrendering ground that has already been secured through Christ.

Exhortation: Put Off the Works of the Flesh

Scripture calls the believer to decisive action. As Paul exhorts in Romans 13:12–14:

"The night is nearly over; the day is almost here. So let us put aside the deeds of darkness and put on the armor of light. Let us behave decently, as in the daytime, not in carousing and drunkenness, not in sexual immorality and debauchery, not in dissension and jealousy. Rather, clothe yourselves with the Lord Jesus Christ, and do not think about how to gratify the desires of the flesh."

This exhortation establishes a decisive contrast between the works of darkness and the life of Christ. The believer is called to reject the patterns of the flesh and to assume a new identity grounded in union with Christ. The command is both negative and positive: to put off the deeds of darkness and to put on the character of Christ.

If the works of the flesh reveal the presence of disorder, the question that follows is how such disorder is overcome. Scripture answers this not through moral reform, but through the life of the Spirit, where the power to overcome the flesh is fully realized.

CHAPTER 16
THE FRUIT OF THE SPIRIT AS EVIDENCE OF VICTORY

In direct contrast to the works of the flesh, the fruit of the Spirit represents the manifestation of Christ's life in the believer. Whereas the works of the flesh are multiple and disordered, the fruit of the Spirit is singular and unified, reflecting the coherent character of Jesus Christ. This fruit is not produced by human effort but is the result of the Spirit's indwelling presence and transforming work. It constitutes the visible evidence that the believer's life is no longer governed by the flesh but directed by the Spirit.

The Nature of the Fruit of the Spirit
Galatians 5:22–23 identifies the fruit of the Spirit as love, joy, peace, patience, kindness, goodness, faithfulness, gentleness, and self-control. These qualities are not independent virtues but interrelated expressions of a single reality: the life of Christ reproduced in the believer. The unity of the fruit underscores that spiritual maturity is not selective but comprehensive, shaping the whole person rather than isolated aspects of conduct.

Each dimension of the fruit functions within the framework of spiritual warfare, both resisting the influence of the flesh and countering the strategies of Satan:

1 **Love** overcomes hatred and division.

2 **Joy** resists despair and accusation.

3 **Peace** dispels fear and confusion.

4 **Patience** endures provocation without retaliation.

5 **Kindness** disarms hostility through grace.

6 **Goodness** confronts moral corruption with righteousness.

7 **Faithfulness** resists deception and compromise.

8 **Gentleness** subdues pride without weakness.

9 **Self-control** restrains the impulses of the flesh.

Where the fruit of the Spirit governs, the flesh is subdued, satanic influence is resisted, and the pressure of the world is overcome.

Walking in the Spirit: The Strategy of Ongoing Victory
The command to "walk in the Spirit" (Galatians 5:16) defines the daily strategy of Christian victory. This walking is not a passive state but an active, sustained dependence upon the Holy Spirit. It involves deliberate obedience, vigilance in the face of temptation, and continual submission to the Word of God.

Victory over the flesh is not achieved through legalism or human effort. The law exposes sin but cannot produce righteousness. Transformation occurs as the believer yields to the Spirit, whose power enables obedience and reorients desire. The Spirit-led life is therefore both freedom and power: freedom from the dominion of the flesh and power to live in accordance with God's will.

Scripture affirms that "against such things there is no law" (Galatians 5:23), indicating that the life produced by the Spirit is never restricted by divine command. The believer is not constrained in holiness but liberated into it, free to pursue righteousness without limitation.

The Defeat of the Flesh Through the Spirit

The relationship between the flesh, the world, and Satan is decisively addressed through the work of the Spirit. The flesh supplies disordered desire, the world reinforces those desires, and Satan exploits them through deception. The Spirit, however, overcomes all three by reordering the believer's inner life and directing it toward God.

Spiritual warfare is therefore not primarily external but internal, taking place at the level of desire, thought, and will. The believer who walks in the Spirit resists the flesh, rejects deception, and stands firm against the pressures of the world. Victory is not defined by the absence of conflict but by the presence of Spirit-governed obedience.

The Call to Mortification

The Spirit-led life necessarily includes mortification, the deliberate putting to death of the deeds of the body. As Romans 8:13 declares, "If by the Spirit you put to death the misdeeds of the body, you will live." Mortification is not an act of self-rejection but a response to the Spirit's work, whereby the believer actively resists and rejects the impulses of the flesh.

This process is continual and Spirit-empowered. It involves discernment, discipline, and perseverance, as the believer aligns conduct with identity in Christ. Through mortification, the influence of the flesh is diminished, and the life of the Spirit is increasingly manifested.

Conclusion: Victory Manifested in the Life of the Believer

The contrast between the works of the flesh and the fruit of the Spirit establishes the decisive distinction between defeat and victory in the Christian life. The flesh produces disorder, division, and death; the Spirit produces life, coherence, and righteousness.

Spiritual warfare is ultimately won or lost in the daily outworking of this reality. The believer who walks in the Spirit overcomes the conflict, manifesting the life of Christ in a world shaped by opposition. Where the Spirit governs, the flesh is subdued, Satan's influence is resisted, and the power of the world is broken.

CHAPTER 17
THE THREEFOLD ENEMY IN SPIRITUAL WARFARE: A TRANSITIONAL SYNTHESIS

Satan, the Flesh, and the World in Galatians 5:16–26

The New Testament presents spiritual warfare as a multi-dimensional conflict involving three interrelated enemies: Satan, the flesh, and the world. This triadic framework provides the organizing structure for this study and reflects the consistent witness of Scripture. Each enemy operates within a distinct sphere, Satan as the external spiritual adversary, the flesh as the internal principle of corruption, and the world as the external system of opposition, yet all converge in their resistance to the reign of God in the life of the believer.

Satan: The External Instigator

The first enemy is Satan, the personal and intelligent adversary who opposes God and His people. Scripture portrays him as active and strategic, employing deception, accusation, and intimidation to undermine faith and distort truth. His aim extends beyond provoking isolated acts of sin to destabilizing trust in God and disrupting obedience through falsehood. Satan does not generate sin as a created reality; rather, he initiates rebellion by exploiting vulnerabilities within fallen humanity. His activity is therefore parasitic, working through distortion rather than creation, persuasion rather than coercion.

The Flesh: The Internal Collaborator

The second enemy is the flesh, the internal dimension of spiritual conflict. Unlike Satan, who operates from without, the flesh resides within, expressing itself through disordered desires that oppose the will of God. It is the inherited condition of fallen humanity and remains present even after regeneration, continuing to exert influence upon thought, desire, and action. As Galatians 5:19–21 demonstrates, the flesh manifests itself through identifiable patterns of behavior that reflect its governing influence. It functions as the point of contact through which external temptation becomes internal consent. What Satan proposes, the flesh desires; what the flesh desires, the will enacts. In this way, the flesh operates as the internal collaborator in spiritual rebellion.

The World: The Environmental Enabler

The third enemy is the world, understood not as creation itself, but as an organized system of values, cultural norms, and ideological structures that stand in opposition to God's authority. The world shapes perception, normalizes sin, and rewards conformity to its standards, creating an environment in which disobedience appears reasonable and righteousness appears abnormal.

Through moral normalization, social pressure, and intellectual distortion, the world reinforces both the deception of Satan and the desires of the flesh. It provides the cultural framework that sustains rebellion and resists transformation.

The Synergy of Opposition

These three enemies do not operate in isolation but function together as a coordinated system of resistance. Satan initiates deception, the flesh internalizes and desires what is proposed, and the world affirms and amplifies those desires through cultural validation. What begins as suggestion becomes desire, and what is desired becomes practice, reinforced by a surrounding system that resists correction.

This integrated opposition explains the persistence and complexity of spiritual conflict. The believer is not contending with a single adversary, but with a network of forces operating across spiritual, internal, and cultural dimensions.

The Spirit as the Decisive Countermeasure

Galatians 5:16–26 presents God's decisive answer to this triadic opposition: "walk by the Spirit." The Spirit does not address these enemies in isolation but confronts them comprehensively. By transforming the inner life, the Spirit subdues the flesh; by grounding the believer in truth, He nullifies deception; and by reordering affections, He disrupts conformity to the world.

The fruit of the Spirit therefore functions as the practical expression of victory. It is the manifestation of divine life within the believer, actively resisting the combined influence of Satan, the flesh, and the world.

Conclusion: From Synthesis to Focus

In summary, Satan is the instigator of rebellion, the flesh is the internal collaborator, and the world is the environmental enabler. Together, they form a unified system of opposition to the lordship of Jesus Christ. Yet this opposition is neither ultimate nor uncontested. Through the work of the Spirit, the believer is equipped to resist, overcome, and live in alignment with the purposes of God.

Having examined Satan and the flesh, the analysis now turns to the third component of this triad: the world. If Satan deceives and the flesh desires, the world shapes and sustains those desires.

Understanding its structure and influence is therefore essential for a complete account of spiritual warfare.

CHAPTER 18
THE WORLD: THE EXTERNAL SYSTEM OPPOSED TO GOD

As redemptive history progresses, exile gives rise to human civilizations organized independently of God. Scripture traces this development through the emergence of cities such as Babel and Babylon, which symbolize collective rebellion against divine authority (Genesis 11:1–9; Revelation 17–18). Drawing on the biblical-theological framework articulated by T. Desmond Alexander in *From Eden to the New Jerusalem*, Scripture presents God's purpose as the formation of a holy people living under his rule, a purpose that culminates in the New Jerusalem.[45]

The World Defined: Biblical Meaning and Scope

Within this canonical framework, "the world" is properly defined not as creation itself—which God declares good and intends to redeem, but as a fallen system of values, allegiances, and structures operating in opposition to God's reign (1 John 2:15–17). As Andreas J. Köstenberger explains in his Johannine theology, the term "world" *(kosmos)* frequently denotes humanity organized in opposition to God and existing within a sphere of hostility toward Him"[46] Friendship with this world constitutes spiritual adultery

---

[45] T. Desmond Alexander, *From Eden to the New Jerusalem: An Introduction to Biblical Theology* (Grand Rapids: Kregel Academic, 2008), 17–23, 263–280.

[46] Andreas J. Köstenberger, *A Theology of John's Gospel and Letters* (Grand Rapids: Zondervan, 2009).

and places the believer in moral alignment with a rival kingdom destined for judgment (James 4:4). As Richard Bauckham argues in his theological exposition of Revelation, the worship of the true God functions as a form of resistance against idolatrous systems, including the deification of political and military power represented by the beast and the seductions of economic prosperity symbolized by Babylon.[47] (See also Chapter 2 on temptation and worship and Revelation 13:17–18.)

In Scripture, *the world* does not merely refer to the physical creation or humanity. Rather, it refers to a *fallen system of values, power structures, and loyalties* organized in opposition to God's rule. The world represents a spiritual order that operates independently of, and often in defiance of, God's will. It is animated by pride, self-exaltation, moral compromise, and hostility toward divine authority...

Scripture explicitly warns against allegiance to this system (1 John 2:15–17), identifying it as fundamentally opposed to the love of the Father and destined for passing away.

The world, therefore, is not neutral. It is a realm of influence that competes for human allegiance, shaping desires, priorities, and identities in ways that are contrary to holiness and obedience.

Scripture frequently uses the term "world" to describe more than the physical creation. The Greek term *kosmos* often denotes an ordered system of values, structures, and loyalties organized in opposition to God and His reign. As G. K. Beale explains in his biblical-theological analysis, *kosmos* functions as a systemic reality, an ordered realm of allegiances and powers that stands in contrast

---

[47] Richard Bauckham, *The Theology of the Book of Revelation* (Cambridge: Cambridge University Press, 1993).

to God's kingdom and operates under hostile spiritual influence.[48] While God loves the created world (John 3:16), believers are warned not to love the world system that operates independently of God (1 John 2:15).

The world, in this theological sense, represents a comprehensive moral and spiritual order that shapes desires, greed, selfish desires, assumptions, and behaviors contrary to divine truth. It includes cultural norms, ideological frameworks, economic priorities, and social structures that exclude God's authority. The world is therefore not neutral territory, but contested ground in spiritual warfare.

The World Under Satan's Influence

Scripture affirms that Satan exercises significant influence over the present world order. Jesus refers to Satan as "the ruler of this world" (John 12:31), while Paul identifies him as "the god of this age" who blinds unbelieving minds (2 Corinthians 4:4). This authority is real but illegitimate, temporary, and subject to divine judgment.

Scripture presents Satan as the temporary ruler of the fallen world system, exercising delegated authority over the nations (Luke 4:6). Yet this authority is neither ultimate nor permanent. At the cross, Jesus announces the judgment of the world has arrived and the prince of this world has been cast out (John 12:31), signaling the decisive overthrow of satanic dominion. Nevertheless, until the final consummation, the world continues to lie under the influence of the evil one (1 John 5:19), creating a contested environment in which redeemed believers live under Christ's lordship while resisting a judged but still active adversary.

---

[48] G. K. Beale, *A New Testament Biblical Theology: The Unfolding of the Old Testament in the New* (Grand Rapids: Baker Academic, 2011), 431–435.

These passages (Luke 4:6; John 12:31; 1 John 5:19) together demonstrate that:

- Satan rules the *world system,* not God's redeemed people

- His authority is *temporary and collapsing*

- Christ's death is the *legal and cosmic eviction notice*

- Final removal awaits Revelation 19–20

Satan's influence does not imply total control over every institution or activity. Rather, it indicates a pervasive orientation away from God that shapes systems and values. The world resists God not merely through overt immorality, but through self-sufficiency, pride, and indifference to divine revelation.

The World and Hostility Toward God

Jesus declares, "If the world hates you, keep in mind that it hated me first" (John 15:18). The world's hostility toward believers flows from its rejection of Christ's lordship and truth. Exposure threatens autonomy; therefore, truth is resisted.

James warns that friendship with the world constitutes enmity with God (James 4:4). This does not forbid engagement with society but condemns allegiance to its values. The world and the church represent two distinct communities governed by opposing authorities.

"Friendship with the world" constitutes open enmity with God. Scripture portrays such friendship not as a neutral association, but as spiritual adultery, a violation of covenantal faithfulness and a betrayal of one's pledged allegiance to the Lord. To love the world is to be unfaithful to God, who stands as the covenant Husband of His people (See Isaiah 54:5; Jeremiah 3:20). The apostolic warning is unequivocal: love for the world and love for God are mutually exclusive (1 John 2:15–17).

This friendship involves the deliberate embrace of the world's *sinful patterns, moral values, and corrupt pleasures*. It reflects a heart that has aligned with a system opposed to God's holiness and rule. Such allegiance is unacceptable to God, for no one can serve two masters (Matthew 6:24). The Lord declares He is a jealous God (Exodus 20:5; Deuteronomy 5:9), not in the sense of insecurity, but in righteous zeal for exclusive covenant loyalty.

A concrete example of worldly friendship is participation in secret orders or lodge-type groups that require unscriptural religious oaths and foster binding spiritual alliances with unbelievers. Scripture explicitly forbids both practices. Christ condemned oath-taking that exceeds simple truthfulness (Matthew 5:33–37), and the apostle Paul warned believers against being unequally yoked with unbelievers in spiritually binding relationships (2 Corinthians 6:14). Membership in such orders inevitably compromises Christian doctrine, weakens godly standards, and divides the believer's loyalty to Christ (See Matthew 6:24; 2 Peter 3:16). A believer cannot maintain fidelity to Christ while submitting to obligations that rival or contradict the authority of God's Word.

The Spirit's Natural Inclination and the Grace of God (James 4:5–6)

The statement, "The spirit that dwells in us lusts to envy" (James 4:5), is difficult to interpret due to the ambiguity of its Greek construction. One plausible understanding is it describes the fallen human nature: the natural tendency of the human spirit, apart from divine grace, is bent toward envy, hostility toward God, and the pursuit of worldly pleasures. This inclination explains humanity's readiness to form illicit alliances with the world (James 4:4).

However, this grim reality is not the final word. Scripture immediately counters human depravity with divine provision: "But He gives more grace" (James 4:6). The very grace that exposes humanity's sinful tendencies also offers transformation. Through humble submission and saving faith in Christ, the believer's orientation is radically altered. Grace breaks the power of envy, restores loyalty to God, and enables a life marked by faithfulness rather than spiritual adultery.

Separation Without Isolation

Believers are called to live in the world without belonging to it. Jesus prays not for removal but protection and sanctification (John 17:15–17). Separation is therefore moral and spiritual rather than geographical.

Scripture commands believers to resist conformity to the world's patterns (Romans 12:2), overcome the world through faith (1 John 5:4), and die to its seductive power through the cross (Galatians 6:14). Such separation preserves holiness while enabling faithful witness.

Paul tells us, "Do not conform to the pattern of this world" (Romans 12:2). The command *"Do not conform to the pattern of this world"* is a foundational principle of Christian theology and spiritual warfare. Theologically, it addresses allegiance, formation, and lordship.

Meaning of "the World" (κόσμος)

In Romans 12:2, "the world" refers to a fallen moral-spiritual system organized in opposition to God. This conceptualization coheres with Johannine usage, where the term consistently denotes humanity in rebellion against its Creator. As D. A. Carson observes in his exposition of John's Gospel, "God's love is to be admired not because the world is so big but because the world is so bad."[49] The world is a value system shaped by rebellion, pride, and self-rule, functioning under satanic influence (See Ephesians 2:2; 1 John 5:19).

The world is:

- A rival kingdom

- A formative power

- A counterfeit moral order

Meaning of "Conform" (συσχηματίζεσθε)

The Greek verb means to be pressed into an external mold. It implies passive adaptation, allowing one's thinking, desires, ethics, and priorities to be shaped by the surrounding system.

Thus, Paul is not merely prohibiting sinful actions; he is warning against:

- Adopting the world's definitions of success

- Embracing its moral reasoning

- Internalizing its assumptions about power, identity, and fulfillment

Theological Contrast: Conformity Versus Transformation

Romans 12:2 presents two mutually exclusive formations:

Worldly Formation	Kingdom Formation
External pressure	Internal renewal
Image of Adam	Image of Christ
Flesh-driven reasoning	Spirit-renewed mind
Temporal priorities	Eternal orientation

---

[49] D. A. Carson, *The Gospel According to John* (Leicester: Inter-Varsity Press; Grand Rapids: Eerdmans, 1991), 205–206.

Conformity shapes behavior from the outside in; transformation renews the believer from the inside out by the Spirit.

Christological Dimension

Jesus refused conformity to the world's pattern:

- He rejected political power without the cross (Matthew 4:8–10)

- He refused popularity-driven kingship (John 6:15)

- He declared His kingdom "not of this world" (John 18:36)

Theologically, Romans 12:2 is a call to cruciform discipleship, to follow Christ's path rather than the world's methods.

Covenant and Worship Theology

Paul frames nonconformity as true worship (Romans 12:1–2). To conform to the world is idolatry because it transfers trust, hope, and obedience from God to the world system.

Therefore:

- Nonconformity = covenant faithfulness

- Conformity = spiritual adultery (James 4:4)

Spiritual Warfare Implication

Within this book's canonical framework, Romans 12:2 identifies the world as a formative enemy that seeks to shape the believer's patterns of thought and allegiance.

As Richard B. Hays argues in his theological reading of Paul, the command in Romans 12:2 calls for a radical reorientation of the believer's imagination and loyalties.[50] Spiritual warfare is not

---

[50] Richard B. Hays, *The Moral Vision of the New Testament: Community, Cross, New Creation* (San Francisco: HarperSanFrancisco, 1996), 33–36.

only about resisting temptation but also about resisting mental and moral assimilation.

The battle is fought at the level of:

- Thought patterns

- Moral reasoning

- Desires and imaginations

- Definitions of "good," "normal," and "successful"

In Summary

"Do not conform to the pattern of this world" means a firm rejection of the fallen value system, authority structures, moral logic, and identity-shaping forces that oppose God's reign, and a conscious submission to transformation by the Spirit according to the mind of Christ.

The Threefold Expression of Worldliness (1 John 2:16)

John identifies three dimensions through which the world exerts influence: "the lust of the flesh, the lust of the eyes, and the pride of life" (1 John 2:16). These categories parallel the temptation narrative of Genesis 3 and the testing of Christ in Matthew 4.

- **The lust of the flesh** refers to disordered bodily desires that seek gratification apart from God.

- **The lust of the eyes** involves covetous longing fueled by sight and imagination.

- **The pride of life** expresses autonomy, arrogance, and self exaltation that denies dependence upon God.

Together, these form a comprehensive framework for understanding worldliness as desire misdirected by rebellion.

Loving the World Versus Loving People

Scripture carefully distinguishes between loving the world system and loving people within it. God's love for humanity motivates the redemptive mission, while rejection of worldliness preserves holiness (John 3:16; 1 John 2:15).

Believers are commanded to love sinners, proclaim truth, and pursue reconciliation without adopting the world's values or practices. Faithful engagement requires discernment, courage, and dependence upon the Spirit.

The Passing Nature of the World

The world system is temporary and destined for judgment. John declares, "The world and its desires pass away, but whoever does the will of God lives forever" (1 John 2:17). Scripture consistently contrasts the fleeting nature of worldly glory with the permanence of God's kingdom (1 Corinthians 7:31; 2 Peter 3:10).

This eschatological perspective fuels perseverance, detachment from temporal idols, and hope rooted in God's promises.

Warning Against Believers and Unbelievers

Do not be yoked together with unbelievers. For what do righteousness and wickedness have in common? Or what fellowship can light have with darkness? What harmony is there between Christ and Belial? Or what does a believer have in common with an unbeliever? What agreement is there between the temple of God and idols? For we are the temple of the living God. As God has said: "I will live with them and walk among them, and I will be their God, and they will be my people." Therefore, "Come out from them and be separate, says the Lord. Touch no unclean thing, and I will receive you." And, "I will be a Father to you, and you will be my sons and daughters, says the Lord Almighty." (2 Corinthians 6:14–18)

In the verses above, Paul exhorts believers not to enter binding partnerships (*unequal yokes*) with unbelief because:

- **Righteousness and wickedness** are incompatible

- **Light and darkness** cannot share fellowship

- **Christ and Belial** represent opposing realms

- **The temple of God and idols** cannot coexist

Paul grounds the command theologically: believers are the temple of the living God. He then weaves together Old Testament covenant promises (Leviticus 26; Isaiah 52; Ezekiel 37) to show that separation is not withdrawal for its own sake, but consecration for divine indwelling and filial relationship ("I will be your Father").

What we all should know:

- **World:** binding alliances with idolatrous systems

- **Flesh:** compromise of holiness through shared loyalties

- **Holiness:** covenant identity grounded in God's indwelling presence

Christological Contrast: World Versus Kingdom of Christ
The world operates on principles of power, self-promotion, and consumption. The kingdom of Christ is marked by humility, obedience, sacrificial love, and truth. Jesus rejected the world's values during His temptation and ministry, choosing obedience over domination (Matthew 4:8–10).

Where the world seeks to ascend, Christ descends. Where the world exalts self, Christ glorifies the Father. Where the world enslaves, Christ liberates. Believers are therefore citizens of a different kingdom, called to embody alternative values within a hostile environment (Philippians 3:20). As R. T. France observes in his commentary on Matthew 5:13–16, "It is important that disciples should both be different and be seen to be different," underscoring that authentic discipleship entails a publicly visible distinctiveness that bears witness to the reality of God's kingdom.[51]

See Table A.8 in the appendix.

The contrast between the kingdom of God and the kingdoms of the world reveals spiritual warfare is a conflict of allegiance and lordship. Satan's strategy is not merely temptation to sin, but seduction into adopting worldly methods to achieve even religious goals. Jesus's rejection of dominion over the kingdoms of the world establishes God's reign cannot be advanced through compromise, coercion, or conformity to fallen systems. The believer's warfare, therefore, requires decisive resistance to the world's values and total submission to the rule of Christ.

Having examined Satan, the flesh, and the world, we now bring these strands together in a unified conclusion centered on Christ's victory and the believer's calling to stand firm.

---

[51] R. T. France, *The Gospel of Matthew*, New International Commentary on the New Testament (Grand Rapids: Eerdmans, 2007), 171–174.

CONCLUSION
KNOWING THE ENEMY, STANDING SECURE IN CHRIST

This study has demonstrated that biblical spiritual warfare is neither peripheral nor speculative, but a central reality within the redemptive drama of Scripture. From Eden to the New Jerusalem, the Bible presents an ongoing conflict between the kingdom of God and forces that oppose His purposes. Yet Scripture is equally clear that this conflict is neither dualistic nor uncertain. God reigns, Christ has triumphed, and the defeat of the enemy is assured.

The New Testament presents Jesus Christ as the decisive answer to the problem introduced in Eden. He is the last Adam, who succeeds where the first failed; the true temple in whom the presence of God dwells bodily, and the victorious King who disarmed the powers of darkness through the cross. In Christ, the dominion of Satan has been broken, the power of the flesh has been condemned, and the authority of the fallen world system has been judged. The cross and resurrection stand as the decisive victory over all three enemies, even as their final removal awaits consummation.

This book has argued that spiritual warfare can be rightly understood only when the believer correctly identifies the three enemies Scripture consistently reveals: Satan, the flesh, and the world. Satan is the personal, external adversary who deceives, accuses, and seeks destruction. The flesh is the internal enemy, the fallen Adamic nature that resists the Spirit and inclines the heart toward sin. The world is the external system of values, structures, and loyalties organized in opposition to God and operating under hostile spiritual influence. These enemies are distinct yet interrelated, forming a coordinated opposition against God's redemptive purposes.

Failure to distinguish these enemies produces confusion and theological imbalance. Some believers attribute every struggle to Satan while neglecting the ongoing reality of the flesh. Others confront moral failure without recognizing the formative power of the world system. Scripture demands clarity: victory requires discernment across all three fronts. To misidentify the enemy is to fight the wrong battle.

At the center of this warfare stands Jesus Christ. The believer does not fight *for* victory, but *from* victory. Through regeneration, believers are transferred from the dominion of darkness into the kingdom of Christ. Through sanctification, they learn to walk by the Spirit and put to death the deeds of the flesh. Through perseverance, they resist deception, endure suffering, and remain faithful until the end. The weapons of this warfare are not human ingenuity, emotional zeal, or mystical techniques, but truth, righteousness, faith, salvation, the Word of God, and prayer.

Romans 8 provides the canonical anchor for this entire theology of warfare. It declares there is now no condemnation for those in Christ Jesus. Assurance is not grounded in moral success or spiritual performance, but in God's decisive action in Christ. Warfare does not reopen the question of judgment; it unfolds within the certainty that judgment has already been rendered in favor of the believer. Though conflict remains real, it is redefined.

The flesh no longer reigns; the Spirit now governs, and perseverance is sustained by divine power rather than human resolve.

Romans 8 also reframes victory itself. Believers are not simply survivors in a hostile world; they are adopted children of God and heirs with Christ. Suffering, opposition, and warfare do not signal abandonment, but participation in God's redemptive purposes. Satan may accuse, the flesh may resist, and the world may oppose, but none of these forces can interrupt the chain of God's saving action. The final word of Scripture on spiritual warfare is not fear, vigilance, or resistance alone; it is assurance. Nothing can separate the believer from the love of God in Christ Jesus.

This study has shown spiritual warfare is not obsession with the enemy, but fidelity to Christ. Scripture never calls believers to fear Satan, reform the flesh, or redeem the world system. Instead, believers are called to submit to God, crucify the flesh, resist the devil, and live as pilgrims whose citizenship is in heaven. The church's power does not lie in cultural dominance, political leverage, or sensational spirituality, but in faithful witness, holy living, and confident hope rooted in Christ's finished work.

T. Desmond Alexander's canonical vision reminds us the story does not end in conflict but in communion. The New Jerusalem stands as the final horizon of spiritual warfare, where God dwells permanently with His redeemed people and where Satan, sin, and the fallen world order are finally removed. Until that day, believers do not live anxiously between defeat and victory, but confidently between justification and glorification.

The enemy is real.

The battle is daily.

The weapons are spiritual.

The victory is secure.

Therefore, knowing the enemy matters, but knowing Christ is everything, stand firm in Him, walk by the Spirit, resist deception, and rest in the unshakable assurance that God preserves His people until redemption is fully revealed.

EPILOGUE
STANDING FIRM, RESTING IN CHRIST

Beloved in Christ,

This book has spoken plainly about enemies that are real, persistent, and often subtle: Satan, the flesh, and the world. Yet it has not been written to stir fear, suspicion, or spiritual anxiety, but so that God's people may walk in clarity, confidence, and peace. Spiritual warfare is not a call to panic; it is a call to stand firm and fight until the end.

You are not alone in this battle, and you are not unarmed. More importantly, you are not fighting *for* victory. You are standing *in* a victory that has already been won. Jesus Christ has faced every enemy you face. He resisted temptation, bore sin, defeated death, and disarmed the powers that once held humanity in bondage. What remains for the believer is not uncertainty about the outcome, but faithfulness in the journey.

When you feel the pull of the flesh, remember that struggle does not mean defeat. The presence of conflict is not proof that God has abandoned you; it is evidence that His Spirit is at work within you. Growth is often quiet, gradual, and forged through perseverance. Do not despise small steps of obedience or moments of repentance. God is patient, and His grace is sufficient.

When the world pressures you to compromise, remember that you belong to another kingdom. You have been called out of darkness into light, not to escape the world, but to live differently within it. Your faithfulness, integrity, humility, love, and endurance bear witness to Christ in ways words alone cannot.

When Satan accuses, whispers lies, or magnifies your failures, do not argue with him; stand in Christ. Your assurance does not rest on your consistency, but on Christ's faithfulness. His cross has spoken the final word over your life. You are forgiven. You are accepted. You are secure.

This book names the enemies so that you will not fight the wrong battles or carry burdens Christ has already borne. But never forget: knowing the enemy matters far less than knowing your Savior. Fix your eyes on Jesus. Walk by the Spirit. Resist the devil. Encourage one another. And rest deeply and confidently in the love of God.

Until the day faith becomes sight, stand firm.

The battle is real, but the victory is sure.

Pastoral Prayer

Heavenly Mighty Father in heaven, hallowed be Your name (Matthew 6:9); we come before You in the name of Jesus Christ, our Lord and Savior (John 14:13–14; 1 Timothy 2:5).

We approach You with reverence and humility, acknowledging that apart from You, we neither see clearly nor walk faithfully (Proverbs 3:5–7; John 15:5). You are holy, righteous, and true (Isaiah 6:3; Psalm 119:137), and Your Word alone gives light in a world darkened by deception and sin (Psalm 119:105; 2 Corinthians 4:4).

Lord, You have not left us without understanding. Through the testimony of Scripture, You have revealed the reality of our enemies, the devil who deceives (Revelation 12:9), the flesh that inclines toward sin (Galatians 5:16–17), and the world that stands in opposition to Your will (1 John 2:15–17). Grant us discernment, that we may not be ignorant of Satan's schemes (2 Corinthians 2:11), nor careless in the face of spiritual conflict (Ephesians 6:11–12).

Search us, O God, and know our hearts (Psalm 139:23–24). Expose every hidden inclination that resists Your will. Where the flesh seeks dominion, bring conviction (Romans 8:13). Where deception has taken root, establish truth (John 17:17). Where the patterns of this world have shaped our thinking, renew our minds according to Your Word (Romans 12:2).

We give You thanks for the victory secured through Jesus Christ. In Him, sin has been condemned (Romans 8:3), the powers of darkness have been disarmed (Colossians 2:15), and the path of life has been opened (John 14:6). Strengthen us by Your Spirit, that we may walk in obedience (Galatians 5:25), resist the enemy (James 4:7), and stand firm in the freedom for which Christ has set us free (Galatians 5:1).

Teach us to live as citizens of Your kingdom in the midst of a fallen world (Philippians 3:20). May our lives bear witness to Your holiness (1 Peter 1:15–16), our words reflect Your truth (Colossians 4:6), and our conduct display the transforming power of the gospel (Matthew 5:16). Let our lives be marked by faithfulness, vigilance, and steadfast hope (1 Corinthians 15:58; 1 Peter 5:8–9).

Preserve us, O Lord, until the day when all enemies are finally defeated (1 Corinthians 15:24–26), when righteousness dwells fully (2 Peter 3:13), and when we behold Your glory without obstruction (Revelation 22:4). Keep us steadfast and watchful, trusting not in ourselves but in Your sustaining grace (Jude 24).

We entrust ourselves to You, confident that He who began a good work in us will bring it to completion in the day of Jesus Christ (Philippians 1:6).

To You alone be all glory, honor, and dominion (Revelation 5:13), now and forever. Amen.

Soli Deo Gloria — To God alone be the glory

— Dr. Jean Marc Joseph

Appendix
Tables

Table A.1

Plague-by-Plague Comparative Table - Yahweh vs. the Gods of Egypt (Exodus 7–12)

#	Plague (Exodus)	Sphere Affected	Egyptian Deity(ies) Implicitly Confronted	Claimed Domain of the Deity	Theological Assertion of Yahweh
1	Water to Blood (7:14–25)	Nile, life source	Hapi, Khnum	Fertility, sustenance, creation from the Nile	Yahweh controls the source of life and renders Egypt's lifeline a source of death
2	Frogs (8:1–15)	Fertility, childbirth	Heqet	Birth, reproduction, and protection of infants	Yahweh alone grants and restrains life; fertility cults are powerless

#	Plague (Exodus)	Sphere Affected	Egyptian Deity(ies) Implicitly Confronted	Claimed Domain of the Deity	Theological Assertion of Yahweh
3	Gnats/Lice (8:16–19)	Dust, land	Geb	Earth, stability	Yahweh commands even the smallest elements; the magicians confess divine superiority
4	Swarms (8:20–32)	Order vs. chaos	Khepri / Set	Creation, order, chaos	Yahweh distinguishes between Egypt and Israel, asserting covenantal sovereignty

#	Plague (Exodus)	Sphere Affected	Egyptian Deity(ies) Implicitly Confronted	Claimed Domain of the Deity	Theological Assertion of Yahweh
5	Death of Livestock (9:1–7)	Economy, agriculture	Hathor, Apis	Fertility, strength, prosperity	Yahweh judges sacred animals and exposes false sanctity
6	Boils (9:8–12)	Health, medicine	Sekhmet, Imhotep	Healing, protection from disease	Yahweh alone wounds and heals; priests and magicians are incapacitated
7	Hail with Fire (9:13–35)	Weather, crops	Nut, Shu	Sky, atmosphere, protection	Yahweh governs heaven and earth; nature obeys His Word

#	Plague (Exodus)	Sphere Affected	Egyptian Deity(ies) Implicitly Confronted	Claimed Domain of the Deity	Theological Assertion of Yahweh
8	Locusts (10:1–20)	Food supply, survival	Osiris, Seth	Vegetation, sustenance, order	Yahweh dismantles false hopes of renewal and abundance
9	Darkness (10:21–29)	Light, cosmic order	Ra, Amun-Ra	Sun, kingship, divine authority	Yahweh eclipses the supreme deity of Egypt and nullifies Pharaoh's divine status
10	Death of the Firstborn (11–12)	Life, lineage, kingship	Osiris, Pharaoh	Afterlife, resurrection, royal divinity	Yahweh alone gives and takes life; judgment reaches the throne itself

Table A.2

Chart / Timeline: Spiritual Warfare from Exodus to Kings

Period	Key Event	Spiritual Warfare Theme	Biblical Passages
Exodus	Plagues on Egypt	Yahweh versus false gods	Exodus 7–12; 12:12
Exodus	Pharaoh resists	War for worship	Exodus 5:1–2
Wilderness	Golden Calf	Idolatry in waiting	Exodus 32:1–10
Wilderness	Fear at Kadesh	Unbelief	Numbers 13:30–33; 14:1–4
Conquest	Jericho	Obedience by faith	Joshua 6:2–5
Conquest	Defeat at Ai	Hidden sin	Joshua 7:1–12

Period	Key Event	Spiritual Warfare Theme	Biblical Passages
Judges	Cycles of oppression	Idolatry to bondage	Judges 2:11–19
Judges	Gideon destroys Baal	Worship precedes victory	Judges 6:25–32
Monarchy	David vs. Goliath	God's honor	1 Samuel 17:45–47
Monarchy	Saul rejected	Disobedience	1 Samuel 15:22–23
Kings	Mount Carmel	True vs. false worship	1 Kings 18:21–39
Kings	Solomon's fall	Compromise	1 Kings 11:1–11

Table A.3

Christological Contrast Chart: Fall of Satan vs. Victory of Christ

Theme	Satan (Isaiah 14:12–17)	Christ (Luke 10:18 Philippians 2:6-11)
Motivation	Self Motivation ("I will ascend")	Humble Obedience
Direction	Attempts to ascend	Willingly descends
Relationship	Seeks equality with God	Submits to the Father
Outcome	Cast down in judgement	Exalted in glory
Authority	Usurped and Temporary	Given by the Father
Effect on Others	Enslavement and destruction	Liberation and Life
Heavenly Status	Fallen from heaven	Seated at God's right hand
Final End	Public humiliation	Universal Lordship

Table A.4

Summary Table: The Names and Titles of Satan

Category	Name / Title	Scripture
Judicial	Satan (Adversary)	Mark 1:13
Judicial	Accuser	Revelation 12:10
Deceptive	Devil	1 John 3:8
Deceptive	Liar	John 8:44
Deceptive	Father of lies	John 8:44
Deceptive	Serpent of old	Revelation 12:9
Predatory	Roaring lion	1 Peter 5:8

Lexical Origin	Primary Function	Framework Emphasis
Hebrew *śātān*	Prosecutor; opponent	Personal instigator
Greek *katēgoros*	Condemnation	Attacks assurance
Greek *diabolos*	Slander; deception	Corrupts truth
Greek *pseustēs*	Falsehood	Distorts reality
—	Source of deception	Shapes worldview
Greek *ophis*	Subtle deception	Historical continuity
Greek *leōn*	Threat; intimidation	Exploits vulnerability

Category	Name / Title	Scripture
Destructive	Murderer	John 8:44
Destructive	Abaddon	Revelation 9:11
Destructive	Apollyon	Revelation 9:11
Cosmic Rule	God of this age	2 Corinthians 4:4
Cosmic Rule	Ruler of this world	John 12:31
Cosmic Rule	Prince of the power of the air	Ephesians 2:2
Cosmic Rule	Ruler of demons	Luke 11:15
Corporate	Rulers of darkness	Ephesians 6:12

Lexical Origin	Primary Function	Framework Emphasis
Greek *anthrōpoktonos*	Death	Sin's outcome
Hebrew *'ăbaddôn*	Destruction	Ruin
Greek *apollyōn*	Destroyer	Annihilation
Greek *aiōn*	Blindness	World system
Greek *kosmos*	Illegitimate rule	External system
Greek *archōn*	Spiritual authority	Unseen realm
Greek *archōn*	Hierarchy	Organized opposition
Greek *kosmokratōr*	Systemic evil	Institutional power

Category	Name / Title	Scripture
Idolatrous	Beelzebub	Matthew 12:24
Idolatrous	Belial	2 Corinthians 6:15
Typological	King of Babylon	Isaiah 14:4
Typological	King of Tyre	Ezekiel 28:12–17
Chaos	Leviathan	Isaiah 27:1
Fallen Glory	Lucifer	Isaiah 14:12
Fallen Glory	Fallen star	Revelation 9:1
Eschatological	Antichrist	1 John 4:3

Lexical Origin	Primary Function	Framework Emphasis
Hebrew/Aramaic	False lordship	Corrupt worship
Hebrew *běliyya'al*	Worthlessness	Moral rebellion
Hebrew (royal oracle)	Pride	Political arrogance
Hebrew (lament)	Exaltation	Economic pride
Hebrew *liwyātān*	Chaos	Disorder
Hebrew *hêlēl*	False light	Self-exaltation
Greek *astēr*	Apostasy	Counterfeit light
Greek *antichristos*	Opposition to Christ	Final deception

Category	Name / Title	Scripture
Eschatological	Lawless one	2 Thessalonians 2:8
Eschatological	Man of sin	2 Thessalonians 2:3
Eschatological	Son of perdition	2 Thessalonians 2:3
Apocalyptic	Dragon	Revelation 12:9
Apocalyptic	Beast	Revelation 14:9–10
Apocalyptic	Little horn	Daniel 8:9–11
Abyssal	Angel of the abyss	Revelation 9:11
Abyssal	King of the abyss	Revelation 9:11

Lexical Origin	Primary Function	Framework Emphasis
Greek *anomos*	Rebellion	Rejection of law
Greek *hamartia*	Transgression	Embodied rebellion
Greek *apōleia*	Destruction	Doom
Greek *drakōn*	Cosmic enemy	Redemptive conflict
Greek *thērion*	Systemic evil	Political power
Aramaic/Hebrew	Arrogant power	Persecution
Greek *abyssos*	Judgment	Imprisonment
Greek *basileus*	Limited rule	Temporary authority

Category	Name / Title	Scripture
Moral	Evil one	John 17:15
Moral	Wicked one	Ephesians 6:16

Lexical Origin	Primary Function	Framework Emphasis
Greek *ponēros*	Moral corruption	Ethical decay
Greek *ponēros*	Harmful intent	Active hostility

Table A.5 (Part 1)
Synthetic Warfare Model
(Daniel - Paul - Ephesians)

Dimension	Daniel 10	Pauline Epistle	Ephesians 6
Realm	Cosmic / angelic	Ministerial / experiential	Ecclesial / practical
Enemy	Territorial spiritual princes	Satan and his schemes	Rulers and authorities
Method	Prayer delayed by conflict	Mission hindered, believers tested	Standing firm in Christ
Human Role	Perseverance and humility	Discernment and endurance	Faithful obedience
Divine Role	Angelic intervention	Sovereign limitation of Satan	Christ's finished victory

Table A.5 (Part 2)
Pauline Theology Chart: Satanic Hindrance

Pauline Text	Mode of Hindrance	Satan's Objective	Divine Limitation	Pastoral/ Theological Implication
1 Thess. 2:18	Physical / strategic obstruction	Prevent apostolic presence and encouragement	Temporary delay only	Mission may be delayed, not destroyed
2 Cor. 2:11	Deception and relational ma-nipulation	Gain an advantage through unforgiveness and division	Believers are warned and equipped	Awareness neutralizes satanic schemes
2 Cor. 12:7	Affliction through suffering	Weaken the apostle	God repurposes affliction	Grace is revealed through weakness
1 Cor. 7:5	Temptation via human weak-ness	Moral failure and spiritual in-stability	Disciplined obedience resists attack	Spiritual disciplines are defensive weapons
Ephesians 6:12	Cosmic spiritual warfare	Resist gospel expansion	Christ's authority is supreme	The church must fight spiritually, not carnally

Table A.6

Genesis 6:1–7 as an Early Biblical Synthesis of Spiritual Warfare

Category	Genesis 6 Textual Indicators	Theological Description	Function in Spiritual Warfare	Christological Resolution (Romans 8)
Satan	"Sons of God" corrupting human order (Genesis 6:1–2)	Manifestation of hostile spiritual influence disrupting creational boundaries and covenant order	Introduces deception, transgression of divine limits, and systemic corruption of God's design	Hostile powers ultimately rendered powerless through the cross; no created power can separate believers from God (Romans 8:38–39; Colossians 2:15)
The Flesh	"Every inclination of the thoughts of the human heart was only evil continually" (Genesis 6:5)	Internal moral corruption rooted in fallen Adamic nature; sin as disposition as well as action	Primary locus of temptation and rebellion; underscores human responsibility	The flesh condemned in Christ's incarnate life; believers empowered to walk according to the Spirit (Romans 8:3–4, 12–13)

Category	Genesis 6 Textual Indicators	Theological Description	Function in Spiritual Warfare	Christological Resolution (Romans 8)
The World	Earth "filled with wickedness" & judgment extending to creation (Genesis 6:7)	A corrupted moral/ spiritual order shaped by collective human rebellion	Normalizes evil, perpetuates violence, and amplifies disordered desires	Creation awaits liberation; bondage to corruption will be reversed in redemptive consummation (Romans 8:19–23)
Divine Response	God " regretted" and was "grieved" (Genesis 6:6)	Anthropopathic expression of divine holiness confronting pervasive evil	Affirms that God responds to sin with both righteous judgment and moral seriousness	No condemnation remains for those in Christ; judgment satisfied through the Son (Romans 8:1)
Redemptive Preservation	"But Noah found favor in the eyes of the LORD" (Genesis 6:8)	Grace perverses a covenant remnant amid universal corruption	Demonstrates that divine purposes advance through grace, not human merit	Those foreknown, called, justified, and glorified are securely preserved in Christ (Romans 8:29–30)

Table A.7

The Threefold Enemy in Spiritual Warfare
A Comparative Chart: Satan—Flesh—World (Galatians 5)

CATEGORY	SATAN (THE DEVIL)	THE FLESH (SINFUL NATURE)	THE WORLD (SYSTEM)
Nature	A fallen spiritual being; personal, intelligent, and malicious adversary	The inherited sinful principle within humanity (sarx)	An organized system of values opposed to God
Primary Location	External spiritual realm	Internal human nature	External cultural, social, and ideological structures
Primary Strategy	Deception, accusation, temptation, intimidation	Desire, corruption, self-indulgence, rebellion	Seduction, normalization of sin, pressure to conform
Biblical Description	Tempter, accuser, liar, adversary	"Works of the flesh" (Galatians 5:19–21)	"The lust of the flesh, lust of the eyes, pride of life"

CATEGORY	SATAN (THE DEVIL)	THE FLESH (SINFUL NATURE)	THE WORLD (SYSTEM)
Method of Operation	Lies, counterfeit spirituality, fear	Habitual patterns of sinful behavior	Cultural influence, peer pressure, false philosophies
Examples in Galatians 5	Witchcraft, hatred, division, deception	Sexual immorality, wrath, envy, drunkenness	Party culture, moral relativism, division, sensuality
Effect on the Believer	Spiritual oppression, deception, discouragement	Weakness, inner conflict, moral failure	Compromise, conformity, loss of holiness
Goal	Destruction of faith and testimony	Domination of the will	Assimilation into ungodly values
Connection to the Other Enemies	Exploits the flesh through temptation	Responds to satanic influence	Reinforces fleshly desires and satanic lies

CATEGORY	SATAN (THE DEVIL)	THE FLESH (SINFUL NATURE)	THE WORLD (SYSTEM)
Scriptural Warning	"Resist the devil"	"Crucify the flesh"	"Do not love the world"
Means of Victory	Authority in Christ; resistance in faith	Walking in the Spirit; self-control	Nonconformity; renewed mind
Primary Countermeasure	Truth of God's Word	Fruit of the Spirit	Holiness and discernment
Defeated By	Christ's finished work	The Holy Spirit	Separation and obedience
Eternal Outcome if Unchecked	Bondage and deception	Exclusion from the kingdom	Spiritual corruption and loss of witness

**Table A.8
Contrast Chart: The Kingdom of God Versus
The Kingdoms of the World
Pride, self-glory, pleasure, ambition (1 John 2:15–16)**

Category	Kingdom of God	Kingdoms of the World
Source of Authority	God the Father established through Christ the Son (Daniel 2:44; Matthew 28:18)	Ultimately offered and administered by Satan (Matthew 4:8–9; Luke 4:6)
Nature	Spiritual, heavenly, eternal (John 18:36; Romans 14:17)	Earthly, temporal, fallen (1 John 2:16–17)
Means of Advancement	Obedience, suffering, humility, the cross (Philippians. 2:5–11; Colossians 1:24)	Power, compromise, coercion, manipulation, violence (Matthew 4:9; Revelation 13:7)
Core Values	Holiness, truth, righteousness, love (Matthew 6:33; Romans 14:17)	Pride, self-glory, pleasure, ambition (1 John 2:15–16)

Category	Kingdom of God	Kingdoms of the World
Method of Rule	Internal transformation—rule in the heart (Luke 17:20–21)	External control—political, social, cultural dominance (Daniel 7:23)
Relationship to Power	Power perfected in weakness (2 Corinthians 12:9)	Power pursued through dominance and force (Luke 22:25)
View of Glory	Glory through obedience and sacrifice (John 12:23–26)	Glory through recognition, honor, and splendor (Matthew 4:8)
Citizenship	Believers transferred into Christ's kingdom (Colossians 1:13; Philippians 3:20)	Humanity apart from Christ remains under its influence (Ephesians 2:2–3)

Category	Kingdom of God	Kingdoms of the World
Leader / Head	Jesus Christ, the Servant-King (Revelation 19:16; Mark 10:45)	Satan, "the ruler of this world" (John 12:31; 2 Corinthians 4:4)
Weaponry	Spiritual weapons empowered by God (Ephesians 6:10–18; 2 Corinthians 10:3–5)	Fleshly, psychological, political, military weapons (Revelation 13:4)
Ethical Demand	Self-denial, holiness, nonconformity to the world (Romans 12:1–2)	Conformity, moral compromise, allegiance to the system (Romans 12:2; James 4:4)
End Result	Eternal life, unshakable kingdom (Hebrews 12:28; Revelation 11:15)	Judgment, destruction, passing away (Revelation 18; 1 John 2:17)

About the Author

Dr. Jean Marc Joseph is a theologian, educator, and evangelist committed to the faithful proclamation of the Gospel and the advancement of biblical theology.

He holds a PhD from Rutgers University and serves as the Founder and President of Dr Jean Marc Evangelistic Ministry, Inc, where he leads teaching, evangelistic outreach, and theological training initiatives.

His work is marked by a rigorous commitment to Scripture within a canonical and redemptive-historical framework. Dr. Joseph integrates careful exegesis, theological precision, and pastoral clarity, equipping believers to understand the fullness of God's revelation from Genesis to Revelation. His teaching emphasizes the believer's identity in Christ, the ministry of the Holy Spirit, the reality of spiritual warfare, and the consummation of God's redemptive plan.

Dr. Joseph is currently developing a multi-volume theological series addressing core doctrines of the Christian faith.

His forthcoming publications include:

- *Know Your Enemies: A Biblical Theology of Satan, the Flesh, and the World*

- *The True Path to Heaven: A Theological and Philosophical Examination of Salvation and Truth*

- *Who Do People Say the Holy Spirit Really Is? A Canonical and Redemptive-Historical Theology of the Person and Work of the Holy Spirit*

- *The Consummation of All Things: A Canonical and Redemptive Historical Theology of the End*

- *Eshet Chayil: The Woman of Valor — A Canonical and Redemptive-Historical Theology of Womanhood*

His writing seeks to bridge the gap between academic theology and practical Christian living, making complex theological truths accessible without compromising depth or doctrinal integrity.

In addition to his writing and teaching, Dr. Joseph is actively engaged in ministry leadership, counseling, and broadcasting, providing biblical guidance to individuals, families, and communities. His work reflects a deep conviction that theology must not remain theoretical but must shape the life, faith, and witness of the Church.

Soli Deo Gloria — To God alone be the glory.

Dr. Jean Marc Joseph
evangelistjeanmarc@gmail.com

9 798995 407508